TABLE OF CONTENTS

CW01508104

INTRODUCTION

Few artists are ever completely absent from popular culture for an extended length of time. Fewer still are known by first name to the general public. Although the name Bruce Springsteen is more likely to be heard alone, say "Bruce" and practically any music enthusiast will know exactly who you're talking about.

Bruce Springsteen has become an unrivaled rock sensation since the release of his first album, Greetings from Asbury Park, New Jersey, in 1973. He's an anomaly in the music industry, a ferociously prolific songwriter, a tireless performer, a musician who forged enduring ties that bind with bandmates (the E Street Band) and a record label he's called home for more than four decades (Sony/Columbia), an artist with the rare ability to court controversy without losing a lot of fans.

And Bruce is everywhere, much like Elvis Presley, his first rock 'n' roller idol, except that Springsteen is alive and well. High Hopes, his eighteenth studio album, debuted at number one in the United States in 2014. Only the Beatles and Jay Z have had more number one singles in the United States than Bruce. It's difficult to go a day without hearing one of his songs on the radio, in a store, or in a restaurant. He continuously tours the world, often performing over a hundred gigs per year. That remark doesn't do credit to Springsteen's live concert, a three-plus-hour whirlwind of rock intensity fueled by improvisation, fan engagement, and freshly worked-up covers as diverse as Mack Rice's "Mustang Sally" and Van Halen's "Jump." (On April 6, 2014, his band added horn arrangements to the latter and performed it for the first song ever to open his Dallas, Texas, show.) Like Elvis and another New Jersey native, Frank Sinatra, he has his own 24-hour Sirius XM station, E Street Radio. From Stephen King's The Stand to T. C. Boyle's collection Greasy Lake & Other Stories to the anthology Meeting Across the River, he appears in literature, not only in works about him but also in writings inspired by him.

Springsteen has also been in a number of films and television shows. His voice is the first one heard in the Oscar-winning documentary 20

BRUCE SPRINGSTEEN
Biography

The Music and Message of Rock 'n' Roll Poet

Josh Aaron Boer

Feet from Stardom, which was released in 2013. Bruce's songs have long been used to great effect in film soundtracks—he won an Oscar for the song he wrote for the critically acclaimed and award-winning Philadelphia, was nominated for his contribution to Dead Man Walking, and won a Golden Globe for his song in The Wrestler. He can most recently be heard in Warm Bodies, a zombie romantic comedy (yes, there is such a thing as a zom-rom-com), and The Place Beyond the Pines, a dark drama. He also made a stunning appearance in Stephen Frears' film adaptation of Nick Hornby's High Fidelity, and he was the subject of the in-depth Ridley Scott-produced film, Springsteen & I, which explored Bruce and his fans' unusual relationship.

His songs have appeared on scripted prime-time television shows such as Sons of Anarchy, Glee, The Good Wife, and The Office. He has performed on Jimmy Fallon's Late Night and The Tonight Show as younger versions of himself for countless humorous song parodies. Those videos, which have been viewed millions of times on YouTube, indicate that, despite his earnestness and the gravity of his job, he is a very hilarious man who does not appear to take himself too seriously.

Springsteen's lyrics are vernacular, with realistic character descriptions, biblical analogies, heartland imagery, and social consciousness woven in. His cultural context is so broad that he may have studied at major American universities, including the Ivy League. Princeton provides a course called Sociology from E Street that delves into "Bruce Springsteen's America." His work was formerly the subject of a history lecture at the University of Rochester. You can study theology at Rutgers via the lens of his lyrics, which may make the most sense to fans who characterize his concerts as a holy experience. You can also pray for him at Portland's Trinity Episcopal Cathedral, which recently hosted a "Bruce Springsteen Eucharist." In July 2014, he gained even more celebrity when he was given his own category on the television quiz program Jeopardy!

His admirers are not the only ones who adore him. The camera still adores Bruce Springsteen, even at the age of 69. With a brooding, craggy face that always seems to catch the proper light, disheveled hair, and an intense gaze that only hints at his uncanny work ethic, he looks like a rock star. Again, like his idol Elvis, he has had distinct, easily recognizable "eras," excluding the overweight, white-jumpsuit Vegas years, of course—a self-proclaimed fitness lover, Bruce has maintained exceptional fitness throughout his life. However, whether photographed in a white tank top and tan during his early Jersey Shore years, bedraggled with his big boho hat or decked out in a suit jacket in the mid-1970s, the red bandana head wrap or bolo tie of the 1980s, or the dark shirts and vests he settled into later on, Bruce Springsteen has always been a compelling subject for photographers. His portraiture is excellent, but he's even better to watch during his sweat-soaked, unexpected concerts, where he's likely to leap up on a piano and crowd-surf.

There's also the issue of New Jersey, where Springsteen was born, raised, and currently resides. The state is mocked for its heavily tolled turnpike, dilapidated cities, and numerous refineries, as well as caricatures of its people and their huge hair, tanning culture, and liberal vowel bending that punctuates the regional accent. Despite the fact that he is an American musician with a global fan following, his name is nearly synonymous with the United States, although in a positive sense. When New Jersey is mocked, it is usually followed by "Yeah, but... what about Springsteen?" Never mind that New Jersey is connected with Meryl Streep, Derek Jeter, Tom Cruise, Anne Hathaway, Shaquille O'Neal, Whitney Houston, Michael Douglas, Bon Jovi, Queen Latifah, Bruce Willis, Yogi Berra, and Martha Stewart, to name a few. Springsteen is the one who gives the state the most hope. He transformed Jersey into song, reflecting its blue-collar families and beach towns' carnivalesque joy and grim reality. He has the ability to make New Jersey romantic and its inhabitants honorable. His surroundings set him apart from other Americana rock artists. There's a sign at the Pennsylvania border that says "where America begins," but for Springsteen and his supporters, New Jersey is and always will be the starting point.

Chapter 1:
My Hometown

The township of Freehold, New Jersey is located about thirty miles east of the Pennsylvania border. Bruce Frederick Joseph Springsteen made his debut on September 23, 1949, at Monmouth Memorial Hospital in nearby Long Branch, and grew up in Freehold. Its schools, churches, communities, and children all contributed to the artist he'd become. It's where the family dynamics that shaped his music and, ultimately, his career took shape. It gave the world one of the most famous rock stars of all time, and the world still loves him.

Springsteen began to show glimpses of the innate gifts that he would cultivate into greatness in Freehold. He was small and modest, but he acquired a physique and a complete dedication to music that proved to be early markers of his exceptionality.

Richard Blackwell, a friend and collaborator of Bruce Springsteen, played conga on his second album, The Wild, the Innocent, and the E Street Shuffle. He went to school with Bruce and knew him from their Freehold neighborhood. Bruce, according to Blackwell, was exceptionally agile, not in a way that suggested superhuman athleticism, but in a way that foreshadowed his hallmark stage maneuvers. Back then, Blackwell, his brother, and pals spent their winter afternoons manufacturing snowballs and throwing them at people walking by and other moving objects, just like bored suburban kids everywhere.

But Bruce loved baseball and still does—he was a right fielder in Little League until the guitar won out over bats and gloves. In 1997, he was inducted into the Little League International Museum Hall of Excellence in South Williamsport, Pennsylvania. He didn't make a career out of baseball, but he did gain one of his biggest singles,

"Glory Days," from his baseball background, as well as numerous hours of onstage banter. He talks about a speedball pitcher in the song based on his real-life teammate and buddy Joe DePugh, who was a good enough player to be invited to try out for the Los Angeles Dodgers in his senior year of high school (despite not making the team). He was also a good enough friend to make fun of Bruce's baseball talents and give him the moniker Saddie.

DePugh claims he and Springsteen have met on occasion throughout the years, most recently at an Italian restaurant in Freehold in 2009. Before they both left, Bruce disclosed to DePugh that his ties to his hometown and its people were more than just a source of inspiration for his job; they were a deep and enduring part of him.

Douglas (Dutch, as he was frequently called) and Adele Springsteen had Bruce as their first child. Virginia arrived a year after Bruce, named after Dutch's sister, who died when she was five years old after being hit by a truck while riding her tricycle. Virginia would subsequently introduce Bruce to George Theiss of the Castiles (the first band with which Bruce recorded), and her marriage would inspire Bruce's song "The River." Bruce was thirteen years old when his parents gave birth to Pamela, who would go on to become an actor and photographer. Adele made certain that her kid understood what was going on during the pregnancy. "She really took me through the whole thing," Bruce says. "We'd be sitting on the couch watching TV when she'd say, 'Feel this,' and I'd put my hand on her stomach and feel my little sister in there." And I had a strong connection with her from the start."

Indeed, the theological virtues of religion—faith, hope, and charity— had a long-lasting influence not only on Springsteen but also on the way he interacted with his audience. He twisted biblical imagery and language into his songs and concerts, and as his conscience grew, he added a deep devotion to exploring social and economic issues. He used his celebrity and fortune to support causes and candidates that, in his perspective, stood for justice. He removed the aspects of faith that were most important to him, prioritizing humanity over theology.

Hope first appeared to him when he was nine, in the guise of a guitar rented for him by Adele. Springsteen informed her that after seeing Elvis Presley on the Ed Sullivan Show, he wanted to be just like Elvis and couldn't see why anyone wouldn't want to be Elvis. When he didn't swiftly grasp the instrument—as each kid does the first time they feel the pinch of guitar strings in their soft, fleshy fingertips—he gave up, only to return to it when he was thirteen. His mother once again assisted him in obtaining his first real guitar, and then his second, the Kent that he'd use in teen bands.

"I'd like to thank my mother, Adele," he said in his acceptance speech for the Rock and Roll Hall of Fame, "for that slushy Christmas Eve, that Christmas Eve—a night like the one outside—when we stood outside the music store, and I pointed at that sunburst guitar, and she had that sixty bucks, and I said, 'I need that one.'" She got me what I needed, protected me, and provided for me on a thousand other occasions. Most significantly, Mom instilled in me a feeling of work as something joyful, that filled you with pride and self-esteem, and that committed you to your world."

Springsteen never put down his guitar again. It was his workhorse, a long-term project that he initiated in a frenzy after months of intense playing in his bedroom. He absorbed himself in it and carried it with him everywhere. He wasn't just pretending to be a loner with a guitar on his back; he was one. He still is in some ways. Friends recall him coming up to parties with girls, drinking, and drugs, only to ignore the fun and vanish with his ax.

Photographs of Bruce as a student at Freehold Regional High School make no impression other than that of a shop class youngster doomed to follow in his father's footsteps and work odd jobs for the rest of his life. His yearbook photo depicts a typical young man with a heavy comb-over and teeth that look to be uncorrected by appropriate orthodontia. Another early photograph depicts a small but cheerful adolescent, full of energy and poised in his seat, ready to bound straight off the page. Academics were not his strong strength, despite the fact that he was innately intelligent and would later devour works by American authors who directly influenced his compositions.

But music was important, even if Springsteen's Kent "sounded awful," according to bandmate Jay Gibson, a member of the Rogues, Bruce's first band as a rhythm guitarist. Gibson claims Bruce was unable to keep it in tune. "All I ever remember telling him was that he needed to get a new guitar because his old one wouldn't stay in tune."

Bruce practiced guitar until he was good enough to join the Castiles, a teenage group managed by local music patron Tex Vinyard that performed in and around Freehold, in 1965. His audition was so rigorous that lead singer George Theiss reportedly asked Vinyard afterward, "Am I still the front man?" Bruce immediately caught on, learning lead guitar sections from bassist Frank Marziotti. Marziotti, who was already in his twenties, was hired by Vineyard primarily because he owned a gas station where the band could practice, but he also served as a model of professionalism and a mentor to the younger players. Bruce, he recalls, was a quick study. "I knew he was a bright kid. "He was a quick learner and a doer," he recalls. Springsteen quickly became a "second " front man, exchanging vocal responsibilities with George. There was rivalry, but "they worked it out between them," Marziotti says.

The Castiles gained a local following after Tex Vinyard invested some money into the band (it was a labor of passion for him, according to Marziotti, and he bankrolled it himself), playing at swim clubs, Elks Lodges, and VFWs, and eventually Cafe Wha? in New York City. "Bruce and the Castiles were one of the better bands," says Joseph Bacenko, a childhood buddy. "Bruce's music, on its own, was good enough to go somewhere." They were quite polished for such a young bunch."

But the deeper Bruce got into music, the more strained his relationship with his father grew. Springsteen's stage banter, another trademark of his live presentation, would be influenced by their disagreements for years.

"He asked me what I thought I was doing with myself," Bruce stated between songs at New York's Palladium in 1976. "We'd always end up yelling at each other." My mother would constantly come storming in from the front room, crying, trying to pull him off me, trying to keep us from fighting... I'd always end up rushing out the back door, away from him. Pulling away from him, yelling at him, telling him, telling him, telling him how it was my life and I was going to do whatever I pleased."

The drama of the Springsteens' Freehold home pervades songs like "Adam Raised a Cain" and "Independence Day," disillusionment and gloom echoing through dark corridors, the musings of a child growing aware in an unenlightened household, a "TV house," as Springsteen once said, with "not a lot of book reading."

Much of the discontent arose from Douglas Springsteen, who brought a lot of grief to his family. His sister's death had thrown an enduring cloud over the household. Douglas dropped out of high school and joined the army, serving in WWII while still a teenager. According to several accounts, he suffered from bipolar disease and was prone to melancholy and fits of fury, and he focused his rage most frequently towards his only son. Steven Van Zandt, guitarist for the E Street Band and longtime Springsteen collaborator, remembers Douglas Springsteen as "scary," but he recognizes that members of the "Greatest Generation" had no frame of reference to deal with their children coming of age in the 1960s.

Douglas struggled to find work in a period when jobs were becoming scarce. Freehold, like Trenton and many other industrial centers, had its own heyday in the mid-twentieth century, with a cannery, an iron foundry, and a branch of the Sigmund Eisner shirt factory, which outfitted the Boy Scouts of America and provided uniforms to the United States government; it was immortalized in Bruce's song "My Hometown."

Springsteen was influenced by Douglas' demons and the terrible times in Freehold for the rest of his life. From Bruce's ambition to be his own boss and live life on his own terms, to his own problems with mental depression many years later, they all influenced his music, the stories he'd come to tell night after night onstage, and even the way he forged a new "family" with the E Street Band.

Chapter 2:
Escape

Springsteen's early work is rife with the yearning to "escape." There was a lot to flee from in postwar blue-collar areas, where families observed the expanding American ideal from a distance but rarely could access it: a declining community, a job with no future, an emotionally complex family, teenage frustration, and the military. When asked what he was rebelling against, the gang leader, like Marlon Brando's Johnny Strabler in The Wild One, answered, "Whaddya got?" Songs like the Animals' "We Gotta Get Out of This Place," which Bruce heard on his mother's kitchen radio, only fueled the fire.

Asbury Park, a coastal village fifteen miles east of Freehold, was the first location Springsteen could genuinely flee. According to Robert Blackwell, kids would cycle there from surrounding suburban communities. Asbury Park was founded in the late 1800s as a tourist town by the Atlantic Ocean, offering beach and boardwalk, but by the late 1960s, it had evolved into an outstanding environment for musicians.

A Thom McAn shoe store was located at 702 Cookman Avenue, a thoroughfare that runs diagonally along the south side of Asbury Park. The Jersey Shore rock 'n' roll sound was germinating just above it. The Green Mermaid Café was one storey higher, and above that was a big space with a short wooden stage that spanned across the far end. From 1968 until 1971, it was the Upstage, an alcohol-free after-hours club where predawn jam sessions were held. Tom and Margaret Potter, husband and couple hairstylists who loved the arts and had a bohemian lifestyle, ran both the café and the club. Carrie Potter-Devening, Tom's granddaughter, claims that the club's concept began in the couple's flat, which was located directly above their beauty store and was decorated with Tom's artwork. The Potters would host parties for their creative friends—photographers, poets, and artists—in their rooftop garden. In contrast to much of Asbury Park's bar environment at the time, it was here that they dreamed of the Upstage, a venue where they could encourage musicians to get together, exchange ideas, and, above all, play original music.

Margaret, Tom's third wife, took up guitar and founded her own band, margaret and the distractions, which became the house band at the green mermaid. The café would close at night, and the upstage would remain open until roughly five a.m. The potters appeared to have placed amplifiers into the wall so that anyone could turn up, borrow a guitar, and plug in and perform. The club's décor, colored with psychedelic paint, evoked hippiedom in San Francisco rather than a beach resort. According to devening, her grandfather even designed a sign for the club that said, leave your anger and hate outside with your booze and drugs.

Ironically, his parents relocated to Northern California around the time Bruce discovered the Upstage. The story goes that they were encouraged to head west by Bruce's girlfriend at the time, but they quickly realized they didn't belong in a bastion of grooviness like San Francisco, and Adele Springsteen was directed to the more provincial San Mateo area after asking someone at a gas station, "Where do people like us live?"

When his parents left the East Coast, Bruce stayed behind, and after convincing his local draft board that he was unfit for service, studying briefly at Ocean County College, and eventually being evicted from his parents' old house, he moved to Asbury Park and found himself in the midst of a musical whirlwind. "Bruce was in the right place at the right time and knew it," Frank Marziotti explains.

"We had a nice community of musicians in that area," says Albee Tellone, Bruce's friend and early roadie. Tellone was active in the Asbury Park music scene, performing at the Upstage and sharing an apartment with Steve Van Zandt and "Southside Johnny" Lyon. "If you needed a bass player or a drummer, there was always someone." Tellone was performing acoustic concerts at the Green Mermaid Café and recalls how "Bruce hung out at the Upstage all the time whenever he didn't have a gig." The Potters' no-alcohol policy didn't bother Bruce because he wasn't a big drinker and never did drugs. Fear of inheriting his father's psychiatric issues motivated him to gain control of his mind. Springsteen, according to Van Zandt, is "the only guy I know—I think the only guy I know at all—who never did drugs." It was unheard of at the time.

Even in a community full of musicians, Bruce Springsteen stood out. He "just had this enormous appetite to play," says Vinnie Roslin, a musician and early bandmate who died in 2012. "He'd play for anyone, anywhere, at any time." He was like a television set with only one channel tuned to 'practice music.'" He didn't look for work because he knew that making music would be his career. Bruce's dedication had only gotten stronger since his days while cooped up with his guitar in his Freehold bedroom. Normal activities, such as finding a place to live—it was catch-as-catch-can for a while—or going to the DMV, fell by the wayside. According to Robbin Thompson, singer of the band Mercy Flight who briefly played with Bruce in the band Steel Mill, at the age of twenty-one, Springsteen still hadn't bothered to get his driver's license—unusual for a kid in highway-heavy New Jersey, and even more unusual for a guy who would write so many songs about cars.

The majority of Asbury Park's bars featured professional cover bands that catered to a Top 40-loving crowd. "They had some great players over there [at the beach bars]," says Tellone. But when the bars closed, the Upstage was just getting started. "Big guys from the scene would come over after their set and just jam," he adds. "Bruce would get them to play, and they'd go through twenty-five-minute songs." Springsteen's blossoming skills as a vocalist, guitarist, and bandleader were on display on the Upstage, and people took note. "He was animated, and he had this look about him, this intangible magnetism, and an honesty about what he did," Thompson adds.

"Even then, as a young guy, he was already one of the best live performers I'd ever seen," Carl "Tinker" West, Bruce's former manager, adds. "He could play the guitar, but he could also sing and communicate with an audience." He lit it on fire, and it worked." Tinker's formula for a successful performance did not include what he thought of the music, whether he enjoyed it or not, or what anyone else thought; instead, he gauged the crowd's reaction. If the audience enjoyed it, he knew he was onto something, and the audience adored Bruce.

Tinker West is a fascinating polymath to this day: a musician, engineer, bona fide rocket scientist (he worked for NASA), and entrepreneur who also happened to be an exceptional surfboard builder. In 1966, he relocated from California to the Jersey Shore and established Challenger East Surfboards in Wanamassa, about a mile and a half northwest of Asbury Park.

Tinker had witnessed the growth of hippie culture and music while living in the San Francisco region, so it's no surprise that he was attracted toward the Upstage, with its whirling Day-Glo paint work and very creative atmosphere. Tinker first heard Bruce play here, and Tom Potter recommended Tinker to Vini Lopez, a drummer who had seen Bruce perform with a band called Earth. Lopez says he had the notion to form a new band after a particularly hot Upstage jam with Bruce.

Lopez claims Tinker had just made him an offer: form an original music band, and he would manage and promote it. Lopez, bassist Vinnie Roslin, keyboardist Danny Federici, and Bruce would make up that band. For a short time, they were known as Child, then Steel Mill. They played so effectively together that "you could hear the other guy breathe," according to Roslin. Their ambitions were high, thanks to Tinker's support.

Tinker had worked in the music industry in California and had a strong interest in it. He also had everything Springsteen and his bandmates needed to get to the next level. His surf store served as the ideal rehearsal place, as well as living quarters and odd jobs. He had a fantastic economic sense—he knew that in order to generate money, artists needed to write their own work and keep their publishing rights. He realized that bands couldn't keep playing the same songs to the same audiences in the same small clubs, and that they needed to travel out of town and tour to properly promote themselves.

To that goal, he bought a tour-worthy truck (which he claims he still has). "We were self-contained," Tinker says of his Steel Mill road travels. "Being self-sufficient gives you an advantage over people who can't." As an engineer, he designed a sound system that improved their live performance and landed them more engagements. He'd earned his moniker while fiddling with hot rods in California, but it seemed to fit when he put together Steel Mill's sound system. "Tinker is some kind of genius-type eccentric guy," Tellone explains. He "took a bunch of blue-collar guys, put them on stage, and made 'em sound good." He inspired them to venture beyond little dives and into larger venues, even touring nationally. He appeared to be the type of person who could do anything and succeed. With the surf business, he was making enough money and had all the necessary resources to fund Steel Mill, and they were soon profitable. It didn't have to be much; Bruce claimed that at the age of nineteen, he could live on twenty or thirty dollars per week. It would take him a decade to make any money.

Finding skilled musicians who were as driven as Bruce was and who could woodshed and travel as needed was a windfall for Bruce. Traveling with the band provided genuine, albeit infrequent, escape, and it blossomed into a lifelong passion for touring. "I like to travel," he explained later. "The idea, to me, is to form a band, write some songs, and tour around people's towns." It's my absolute favorite. It's like being at a circus. You just wheel along, walk into someone's town, and bam! It's a heart-to-heart conversation. Something bad can happen to you, and it can also happen to them. You believe you have the ability to make a difference in someone's life. All I'm trying to do is wake others up and do the same for myself."

Tinker was a businessman first and foremost, but he genuinely enjoyed music and cared about his friends. He wasn't just following them; he was riding with them as part of the squad. He made sure they had food, gas, and hotel, even arranging for the band to stay with his friends on a long trip to California. Tinker and Bruce rode in his truck, followed by the rest of the band. Tinker put Bruce behind the wheel for some much-needed driving practice when he became fatigued. (According to Tinker, girls had previously driven him about, so he never had to learn.) During their West Coast visit, they recorded a demo with Bill Graham of the Fillmore. "Graham offered him a record deal, but he demanded complete control over the publishing." "I said no," Tinker explains. "Publishing is the equivalent of a musician's retirement." That, I believe, should be preserved."

Tinker was also a terrific taskmaster. He insisted on rehearsals beginning early in the morning and lasting into the evening, when his surfboard manufacturing closed for the night. He could keep track of the band's progress because he was at his shop all day. Critics who claim that the "poet of the working man" never worked may be unaware that Springsteen performed some surfboard detailing at the shop, and they have clearly never bothered to perfect the craft of songwriting.

Tinker, a musician himself, heard Springsteen's budding magic as he relentlessly pushed at his craft in Texas Vinyard's Freehold garage. Tinker describes Bruce as "constantly writing songs." "He was driving around writing a song." And the music told stories about things. It progressed. Bruce wrote these songs on a regular basis; he was always sitting around with an acoustic guitar, composing lyrics and trying to piece things together. When he finally got it to work the way he expected it to, they'd fiddle with the music until they got it." Tinker, as a craftsman, understood. Writing songs can be compared to hewing surfboards in terms of shaping storylines out of piles of words and cutting out musical arrangements.

Tinker oversaw the Steel Mill from 1969 until 1971. They gained a large following on college campuses and opened for national performers. However, when visiting his parents, Bruce saw Van Morrison perform in San Francisco and had an epiphany, or perhaps understood that he had reached his limit in a hard rock band. Morrison infused R&B into his folk rock, and this, along with his horn band and backup vocalists, influenced Springsteen. Other artists, including Leon Russell and the late Joe Cocker, were pushing the frontiers of rock in similar ways, but it was Morrison's live presentation that showed Bruce how he wanted to present his music.

Albee Tellone recalls Bruce telling the band members that they needed to alter things up. "He said, 'Hey, I need to try something like this,'" says Tellone. "He basically just told everybody, 'Look, I'm done with this, I'm going to start something new; if you want to join along with me, you can.'"

"Everybody talks about the Asbury sound," explains Vini Lopez. "Well, that's the start of it, the transition from Steel Mill to that band."
That was far from the case. The massive concert that Bruce envisioned at the time would serve as the framework for an unrivaled act that would span more than four decades and provide joy and even hope to millions of fans worldwide. It would become "part circus, dance party, political rally, and big tent revival," according to Vini Lopez. Fans can describe it as a house party or even a religious experience.

"He called it 'the big band,'" Tellone explains. "They didn't know what to call it, because Steel Mill had the connotation of being a loud, crunching" band, however "this was kind of a soul band." 'Why don't you just give it your name?' Steve [Van Zandt] and I suggested one day. You're writing the songs, you came up with the idea, and you're doing the arrangements.' 'Well, I don't know, that's sort of an ego trip, isn't it?' he asked. 'Do it, believe us, it'll work,' we urged. Tellone claims that after some time of tossing around stupid names, the Bruce Springsteen Band was born.

Springsteen began building a ten-piece band, but they were far from ready when Tinker received a request to play for the Allman Brothers Band at the now-defunct Steel Mill. "Give me Springsteen, I don't care how," Tellone recalls the club manager saying. So Bruce recruited a group of his buddies to construct the stop-gap Dr. Zoom and the Sonic Boom, which was all about turning the Upstage mood into a major event. "Because they'd be opening for the Allman Brothers, who had two drummers and two lead guitarists," Tellone explains, "Bruce and Steve decided to match that and go two steps further by adding] two keyboard players and two sax players."

"Dr. Zoom had everyone we knew in the band," Lopez explains. "Two of everything: two drummers, two bassists, two guitars, two singers, two baton twirlers, ringmaster, and two Monopoly players—Big Danny [Gallagher] and Big Tiny both played Monopoly."

According to Tellone, Monopoly was often played at Van Zandt's apartment, albeit they put their own spin on the game that mirrored the shifting vibe of Asbury Park at the time. "He and his musician friends liked to play a rough version of Monopoly, adding handmade cards to the Chance and Community Chest piles." If you drew the Race Riot! card, all of your residences and hotels would be destroyed."

The times had changed. The Upstage was closed in 1971. The same upheaval and violence that was erupting in places around the country were driving people away from Asbury Park. Bruce had learned to call the road home, which he would do for the rest of his adult life. Steel Mill was finished, and it was time to go forward.

Tinker believed that if a commercial effort didn't earn money, it wasn't worth pursuing, and a ten-piece band was a deal breaker. It wasn't "economically feasible" to travel that route, he claimed. He had brought Bruce as far as he could despite playing congas in Dr. Zoom and the Sonic Boom. He introduced Bruce Springsteen to producers/managers Mike Appel and Jim Cretecos. Bruce's next "escape" would be from obscurity.

Chapter 3:
Great Expectations

Springsteen's two-year Working on a Dream tour concluded on November 22, 2009, in Buffalo, New York, with something the band had never done before and had pledged to do only once: play Greetings from Asbury Park, N.J., Bruce's raw but promising debut album, from beginning to end.

Before the show, Bruce and his bandmates formed a reflection circle with their hands joined. "I wouldn't want to be anywhere else in the world right now other than here with you guys," Bruce stated. Jon Landau, his lifelong friend, manager, and producer, stood to his right.

A man with thick white hair and steely blue eyes stood on the other side of Bruce, grasping his left hand. Mike Appel, his former manager and producer, was both an orchestrator of coups that catapulted Springsteen to fame and a litigant who kept him in court and barred him from entering a recording studio on his own during the crucial year following the release of Born to Run, his biggest success at the time.

Appel was anathema to many Springsteen fans. On that particular occasion, Bruce was an invited visitor. Bruce had flown Appel and his kid to Buffalo on a private aircraft with the E Street Band, invited him backstage, and devoted the event to him as he told the enthusiastic audience about the genesis of his first album. "It was a miracle. "This was the record that took everything from zero to... one," he joked with the audience. He explained how Appel's "incredible talking" secured him an audition with John Hammond, Columbia's famed producer who had signed Bob Dylan. "I'd like to thank the man who got me in the door. Mike Appel is here tonight— this is for you, Mike. We've never done it before [perform the entire album]... "I hope we can pull it off," Bruce added.

His connection with Apple is, in some ways, another of Bruce's paradoxes. Appel's aggressive tactics created numerous opportunities while nearly costing him a big business agreement and cost him a large amount of time and money. A lesser artist would have been destroyed. Hammond was so irritated by the relentless manager that he claims he was "ready to hate Bruce" when he strolled into his office in the spring of 1972 with an uncased guitar. "Appel is as offensive as any man I've ever met," adds Hammond, "but he's utterly selfless in his devotion to Bruce." Later, Appel would push Time and Newsweek against each other for a cover story on Bruce Springsteen, nearly losing both. Even Appel admits that he had no idea what was going to happen leading up to the week of October 27, 1975, until the magazines with Bruce covers hit the newsstands.

It's amusing to speculate on Bruce's fate if he hadn't signed the deal with Appel on the bonnet of a car in a dark parking lot, according to an apocryphal narrative. Springsteen's graceful performance in Buffalo nearly four decades later says a lot about him. Another Roman Catholic, Alexander Pope, stated that forgiveness is divine, however it may be easier to forgive someone when you've risen to the pinnacle of your field and the other guy hasn't.

But, for all his zeal and drive, Bruce had a Zen-like way of welcoming people in, letting them go, and bringing them back again. Musicians were a means to a purpose, which was to create the best rock records and put on the greatest rock shows ever, and possibly, like many entertainers, to be infinitely loved. But musicians were also a family, and like any family, even if you don't see one another for a while, you're always connected. He disbanded the E Street Band in 1989, only to reassemble it a decade later. Over the years, he offered gigs, royalties, benefit concerts, and other acts of kindness and acknowledgment to many of the people who departed his orbit, either on their own or at his request. Beyond the live act, beyond songs that speak to them and musical hooks that affect them, what fans latch onto is the awareness that beneath one of rock's greatest showmen is a knowing heart.

Appel claims that through monitoring his young signee, he discovered that Bruce had figured out something that Apple had missed very early on. In 1974, keyboardist David Sancious, whose house on E Street inspired the band's name, and drummer Ernest

``Boom" Carter signed their own record deal with Epic, a division of Columbia Records. "It really hurt me when he [Sancious] left," Appel said as a guest DJ on Sirius XM's E Street Radio. "I was completely insane when I found out." "The guy's a genius," he said to Bruce. When you hire a fantastic keyboardist like this man, he discovers great small pieces that make your songs even more magical than they already are. He gives another layer to these tunes that would be lost without him." Furious at the prospect of losing Sancious, he called Epic and attempted to scuttle the purchase.

Appel had gotten Bruce a fantastic ten-album contract with Columbia thanks to his "incredible talking," or possibly because of it. "The kid knocked me out," adds Hammond. They both imagined Bruce as a solo artist, the heir apparent to Bob Dylan, with lyrics so superb he'd just need an acoustic guitar.

Bruce, on the other hand, had different plans. He had his band of guys, some of the best musicians on the Asbury Park bar scene: Vini Lopez, who inspired the "madman drummer" line in "Blinded by the Light" (his nickname would become "Mad Dog"); Clarence Clemons, the sax player, his six-foot-five stature earning him the eternal moniker: the Big Man; Garry Tallent, the bassist who would become the longest running E Street Band member; and Sancious, the Springsteen and his musicians had formed a bond while performing live, and he believed that he could make the record he desired with them. Bruce had a bright future ahead of him, and he was bringing his buddies with him.

There was some disagreement about what was included on the record. Springsteen and Appel's colleague Jim Cretecos (who would leave that year, allegedly cashing out his half of Bruce's publishing for $1,500) intended to record a rock album, but Hammond and Appel preferred an acoustic album. The label also wanted a shot of its scruffy, windblown troubadour for the cover, but they wouldn't receive it until the second album. Before the needle ever touched the turntable, Bruce insisted on a vintage postcard he'd discovered that encapsulates every bit of Asbury Park's nostalgic enchantment and classic Americana spirit.

According to music business billionaire Clive Davis, who wrote about Springsteen in his 2013 biography, The Soundtrack of My Life, the only thing missing from the album's first iteration was a smash song. Davis, who was the head of CBS Records at the time, returned the album to Bruce and asked him to come up with something more. Bruce went home and looked through a rhyming dictionary for ideas. "I went to the beach and wrote 'Blinded by the Light' and 'Spirit in the Night,'" explains Springsteen. "That was a wise decision. They turned out to be two of my favorite tracks on the album."

Dynamic live performers may sound flattened in the studio, and Greetings is no exception. But it had the hallmarks of a rising music star: passionate vocals, lush orchestration, rhythms reminiscent of feet moving across sand and pounding waves, and a sense of place. Greetings sounded like a lost and dirty weekend "down the shore"— an instant sign if someone is from out of state, because they'll say "down to the shore."

The two late song additions hinted at potential chart success. Manfred Mann's Earth Band would take "Blinded by the Light" to number one on the Billboard Hot 100 several years after Greetings was released; if you were alive in 1976, there was no avoiding the oversized, psychedelicized version of Bruce's song, which was so prevalent that the casual listener didn't know who wrote it. Springsteen established some of his most memorable characters on "Spirit in the Night," which are repeated by the backup vocals of the allegorical group in their natural habitat: Wild Billy, Hazy Davy, Crazy Janey, Killer Joe, G-Man, and narrator Mission Man, as they journey to Greasy Lake for some misadventure. The sparse arrangement is the result of the song being recorded after most of the original players had left, giving "Spirit" an appropriately haunted atmosphere. Vini Lopez and Clarence Clemons were the only survivors. Except for some piano by studio musician Harold Wheeler, Bruce performed all of the other instruments.

Lester Bangs, the legendary rock writer, gave Greetings a generally positive review in Rolling Stone, citing influences such as Van Morrison and The Band and praising Springsteen's Jersey pride ("Old

Bruce makes a point of letting us know that he's from one of the scuzziest, most useless, and plain uninteresting sections of Jersey") and his dazzling wordplay ("What makes Bruce totally unique and cosmically surfeiting is his words. What a smorgasbord of language! He's stuffed more of them into this album than any other record released this year, but that's okay since they all fit snugly").

Greetings from Asbury Park, New Jersey caused a ripple rather than a splash when it was released in January 1973. Springsteen wasn't quite the barn burner he was on stage. He did, however, live true to the music industry cliche that it takes ten years to create your first album and six months to create your second. Bruce stunned critics with The Wild, the Innocent, and the E Street Shuffle in September 1973, revealing his rising skill in song arrangement. It highlighted Sancious' enormous chops. The Wild, the Innocent was jazzier, funkier, even punkier—smarter. The "shore rat" demonstrated that he had spent some time in New York City. It was a lengthy bus ride and a world apart from Asbury Park, but Bruce was eager to take up the atmosphere and incorporate it into a song.

"We did the first album in a week, basically all in one take." "The second album took longer," Lopez admits, "but it was also a better time." "There's priceless stuff there." Like the yelling in 'The E Street Shuffle.' We're having a party. We were definitely drinking, yelling, and hollering. We weren't just standing there pretending. We drank tequila and had a good time."

Lopez would be asked to leave the band prior to the release of the next album. He and Mike Appel clashed about money, management, and Lopez's sense of ownership in the enterprise. "I started the band, and now I'm getting crap from Mike." It didn't sit well with me. "I spoke up," he explains. Lopez was dismissed after a fight with Appel's brother. However, on The Rising tour in July 2003, and on several occasions thereafter, Bruce greeted Lopez backstage at the Meadowlands with a hug and a request to perform "Spirit in the Night," which he accepted. "That was something, going back to play," Lopez adds. "I never expected Giants Stadium. That was the first time I had played with them in thirty years." He'd perform with the band again in 2009 at the Philadelphia Spectrum and again in

2012 at the Meadowlands. Lopez and the rest of the E Street Band were inducted into the Rock & Roll Hall of Fame in 2014. He probably didn't expect it either.

Boom Carter replaced Lopez and stayed just long enough to perform on Bruce's magnum work, "Born to Run," widely regarded as one of the best and most lasting rock songs of all time. He'd play it at practically every non-solo show he ever did, turning on all the house lights and unifying an arena full of people every time.

Springsteen was plagued by his own ambition and perfectionism while creating this exultant homage to escape and the album of the same name. He desired—no, required—that it be unrivaled. His job was also at stake. While the first two albums received favorable reviews, they did not strike a chord with the general public. As rumors arose that Springsteen may be dropped, Columbia had signed a new star, Billy Joel, and was enthusiastically pushing him. Moving to Long Branch and living alone for the first time, he wrote songs under immense pressure. "It was the most horrible period of my life," he recalls. "I was born, grew old, and died while making that album."

In 1974, Bruce and his band were still performing at colleges, tiny theaters, and taverns. They arrived at the Harvard Square Theater on May 9, two days before they began the first phase of recording Born to Run, to open for Bonnie Raitt. That night, there were two performances. Michael Atherton, a Boston baker and musician who slipped tape equipment into the theater, captured the early show. Years later, his tape surfaced and made its way into Bruce Springsteen's "From Asbury Park to the Promised Land" display at the Rock and Roll Hall of Fame and Museum, where museumgoers could listen in on what he heard that night via digital stream. "It was the greatest band concert I've ever seen," recalls Atherton, "completely together, completely refined, the dramatic intent clear from beginning to end."

Rock critic Jon Landau, one of Rolling Stone magazine's founding writers and a record producer who'd worked with Livingston Taylor, the J. Geils Band, and the MC5, praised the late show. Landau's audacious declaration, which became one of the most widely cited pieces of music criticism ever, would change his life, Bruce's life, and rock history. "I saw the future of rock 'n' roll, and its name is Bruce Springsteen," he wrote in his review of the show for Boston's alternative weekly the Real Paper. He'd met Bruce briefly a month ago at Charlie's Bar in Cambridge, where the party was staying for four nights. They became friends, talking on the phone, sleeping on each other's couches, going up late into the night, and exchanging ideas about rock 'n' roll, which they both adored.

Bruce's ambition for his third album mirrored Landau's oft-quoted (and misquoted) statement. "I wanted to make the greatest rock record that I'd ever heard," says Springsteen. "I wanted it to sound massive, to grab you by the throat and force you to take that ride, to pay attention—not just to the music, but to life, to being alive." The acoustic elements had to be massive. To that goal, Springsteen and Appel borrowed elements of Phil Spector's Wall of Sound recording techniques from a former collaborator of the legendary producer. The words had to be equally captivating; Bruce claims he wrote and wrote and peeled away every cliché from the songs until he felt genuine emotion. What he sought and received was not only the success he craved, but something so life-affirming to music fans that it continues to inspire devotion around the world.

Born to Run took fourteen months to finish, split into two halves. During the initial phase, the band continued to tour and recorded without any session musicians, a somewhat haphazard method that didn't totally succeed. By October 1974, Springsteen had begun discussions with Landau regarding the role of producer, inviting him to the second session in 1975 and finally signing him on as a co-producer alongside Appel and himself. Landau immediately stepped up their game, suggesting that they relocate the project from 914 Sound Studios in Rockland County, New York, to the Record Plant near Times Square, which was better suited to making the big rock record that he and Bruce had in mind and was a little closer to the musicians who lived down the shore.

The stories of how Born to Run came to be belie its happy ending, with tales of Bruce's laborious quest of perfection, retake after retake, and grueling all-nighters in which some of the musicians would fall asleep mid-session. "The album became a monster," adds Bruce. "It desired everything. It simply ate everyone's life." In contrast, the record marked the beginning of some of Bruce's most crucial professional connections. Landau was a significant influence. He raised the bar in terms of professionalism. He enlisted the help of skilled engineer Jimmy Iovine, the Brooklyn-raised son of a longshoreman who had worked with John Lennon and done odd works for Phil Spector. Landau also gave Bruce the appropriate amount of prodding, which is the only way to get a perfectionist to accomplish something, asking him to "do it your way, but do it," as Springsteen recounts. Steve Van Zandt returned to the fold as a guitarist, helping to extract what was inside his old friend's head and get it onto tape, even singing the horn parts so that the famed session men Michael and Randy Brecker could interpret it on tape. And, after tryouts that lasted so long that Mike Appel walked out, Bruce found the ideal replacements for Sancious and Carter—Roy Bittan and Max Weinberg, who both played on the record and are still with him to this day.

Springsteen performed a remarkable ten-show (five nights, two performances each) run at New York City's Bottom Line a few weeks before the album's release. Fans were treated to fresh music. Music critics and deejays received a sneak peek at the singer-songwriter's metamorphosis; some who had dismissed him were won over, which was crucial in releasing the album. Each event began with the band's R&B-driven behemoth "Tenth Avenue Freeze-Out," and Bruce went up from there, climbing on the piano and patrons' tables in the relatively tiny, 400-seat venue.

Born to Run peaked at number three on Billboard's Top 200, fulfilling Springsteen's aim of having his songs played on car radios, which they have done ever since. It has since appeared on numerous lists of notable recordings, including the number eighteen spot on Rolling Stone's "500 Greatest Albums of All Time," a spot in the NPR 100—"the 100 most important American musical works of the twentieth century," and, in 2003, the Library of Congress's National Recording Registry.

Born to Run was, in many ways, Bruce's pivotal moment between adolescence and adulthood. The album offers one of the most vivid expressions of adolescent emotion: love, lust, loneliness, and, most importantly, the heart of adolescent dreams: leaving your hometown. Springsteen recreated iconic American themes from his boyhood in the 1950s—cars, chrome, and girls—by stripping them of their retro components and recasting them in a timeless manner.

The album was also transitional in terms of band personnel and management, with the exits of David Sancious and Bruce's longtime friend Vini Lopez, as well as the aftermath of Bruce realizing he had signed a terrible management arrangement. "The initial contracts were naive, rather than evil," he said. Worse than the financial disadvantage was the creative autonomy he'd given to Apple, who had "the power to decide all the essentials about how we recorded, who we recorded with," according to Bruce. "It wasn't about money; it was about control, about who would be in charge of my work and my work life." I decided early on that was going to be me." He wouldn't walk into a studio if he couldn't make his own judgments regarding the recording process, and he didn't for a year.

He was also a prolific writer. He moved into a house in Holmdel, New Jersey, where he could create as much noise as he wanted at any time. He called his guys together for daily practices. With the threat of a lawsuit hanging over their heads, they started working on another record.

Chapter 4:
Darkness

Springsteen talks with BBC2's Bob Harris backstage after his August 25, 1978 gig at the Veterans Memorial Coliseum in New Haven, Connecticut, for The Old Grey Whistle Test TV show. His wiry physique is slightly stooped down in a huge chair, sweat-soaked and hair mussed. A tape boombox, a lamp with a fake tree trunk bottom, and a huge can of Hawaiian Punch on ice are next to him. Bruce is not a big drinker, but in his early years, he lived on junk food so much that his bandmates had to persuade him to have a proper meal every now and again. His voice is hoarse, and he seems exhausted. During live performances, he gives his all and there's almost nothing left, but his hand movements become expressive when he talks about recording his latest album, Darkness on the Edge of Town. "It was a lot more fun than Born to Run," he says. "Born to Run was really... that was really difficult."

Springsteen struggled to find his place in the world, caught between his old life and newfound fame. Darkness' creation "was a survival thing," he explains. "I had a reaction to my good fortune after Born to Run...." My greatest concern was that success would alter or lessen that aspect of myself." He believed that reconnecting with his history was critical to not lose himself.

If Born to Run marked Bruce's commercial crossroads, Darkness marked his transition into adulthood. As he approached the crucial age of thirty, he had outgrown juvenile themes and began to relate more with the people in his past—the ones who had lived lives he had worked so hard to avoid. "I was trying to write music that felt angry and rebellious, but also adult," explains Springsteen. He'd also had to mature quickly as he faced the dispute with former manager Mike Appel. The year he spent fighting for his artistic future left a pall over him, and he felt hurt fighting someone so close to him. "The loss of Mike's friendship was a terrible loss," explains Springsteen.

A video of Bruce and Steven Van Zandt performing an early version of "Sherry Darling" shows that there was still fun to be had despite all of the failures. Springsteen knocks out chords and sings while Van Zandt stands next to him, pummeling a piece of furniture with a pair of drumsticks and adding spicy harmonies where appropriate. When they're finished, Bruce stands up and jokes that it's "the one and only performance of this phenomenal song you've captured on tape."

"Sherry Darling" did not feature on Darkness, although it did emerge on Bruce's next album and in his live performance over the years.

The majority of the songs created during the album's production, perhaps seventy, according to Jimmy Iovine, with forty or fifty recorded according to Max Weinberg, did not make the cut, but this was part of Springsteen's creative process. "What would happen is that I'd write a song, and then I'd write like four songs," he explains to the post-gig camera centered on him. "And then the fifth song, which would be like song number two on the album, would be a progression up." And then I'd create four more songs until I got to the ninth tune, which was like the third song on the record. Meanwhile, all of these other songs would be filler to help you get to your destination. So that's how the record was created."

The approach was significantly different from the previous three albums. "Basically, the first ten good songs you write, you put them out, and that's your record," Steven Van Zandt explains. "Well, that process would end forever." Springsteen, instead of going into the studio until he could do it on his own terms, became a songwriting juggernaut, cranking out material like a Brill Building professional, even if he couldn't utilize it. His two biggest hits during this time were songs he gave away: "Fire," to R&B quartet the Pointer Sisters, and "Because the Night," to punk poet Patti Smith. "If he thought something was going to be a hit but didn't want to be represented by that hit, he'd just leave it off the record," explains co-producer Jon Landau.

Springsteen's "magic notebook," as Roy Bittan dubbed it, was jam-packed with ideas, lyrics, and songs that would be written and rewritten over and over again, amazing tunes that might or might not end up on the record. It became a symbol for the band, indicating that more work was on the way. "It was a learning process for all of us, both frustrating and funny at the same time," Max Weinberg explains. "We wanted to make a great record." Every time we played, we tried to create something significant and lasting. We were experimenting with so many different things. Bruce would rehearse us for several days on a tune before tossing it out. He had a plan, albeit it wasn't always evident to the rest of us."

The weeks they spent alone trying to obtain the ideal drum sound— including hours hammering the snare and days moving the drum kit around—were agonizing at times. Weinberg, on the other hand, was adamant. He, like Bruce, had grown up watching Elvis on television; however, it was his drummer, D. J. Fontana, who piqued Max's interest. "I think anybody who wanted to make a career out of rock 'n' roll music had a chance," he says. "That was my big moment."

The meticulous attention to detail demanded complete immersion from everyone. "The problem was this: I fantasized about these huge sounds, and so we went to pursue them, but they were always bigger in my head," Springsteen explains. "So we were constantly chasing something that was somewhat unattainable."

"We were typically recording from three o'clock in the afternoon to three o'clock in the morning, five days a week," Weinberg explains. "There was this constant flow of material—and a lot of takes." Everyone was frustrated at times, both individually and collectively, but you wanted to perform well for Bruce. There was a crucible quality to it: under strain, we evolved as individuals and as a band."

During this time, Bruce also worked hard to overcome the perception that he was a hyped-up record label construct, as some critics had speculated when Born to Run was launched. "We had to re-prove our viability on a nightly basis, by playing, and it took many years," he says, but his new album will demonstrate that Born to Run, the album that made him famous, was merely the beginning.

Springsteen's prolific writing varied in style and theme, but his goal for this album, portraying this moment of his life and the world around him, was darker than anything he'd done before. He was looking for "something like a tone poem" and "apocalyptic grandeur," according to him. He found a way to celebrate the working men and women he'd grown up among while working out his own feelings of dread, powerlessness, and despair in the songs—sometimes succumbing, sometimes swinging at them like a fighter fighting to the death. Though he claims he was attempting not to be self-referential at the time, it's evident from the first track, 68, that he's dealing with make-or-break issues.

Anyone who has ever felt hollow at home can relate to Darkness on the Edge of Town: the father who "walks these empty rooms looking for something to blame" in "Adam Raised a Cain," the boy who walks "the darkness of Candy's hall," and the "sadness hidden in that pretty face" of the girl he desires in "Candy's Room." It's an introspective sketch of rage. In those halls, the despair that tormented Springsteen at times throughout his life coexists with the consequences from a year of worry about his own destiny.

Darkness wasn't just an emotional fork in the road for Bruce; it was also a musical one. He began to explore beyond New Jersey for heartland themes. "I started listening to country music, which I hadn't really done before," adds Springsteen. "I really connected with Hank Williams for the first time." What I appreciated about it was that country music addressed grownup issues." He and Landau began discussing using music to create visuals, "the sound of the picture," as Landau puts it, and pulling inspiration from country music helped them do it.

Springsteen was also very conscious of his surroundings. It was 1977, the year punk rock blossomed, and he was influenced by it as well. He had been a fan of proto-punk since the early 1970s, when he was living in New York and performing at Max's Kansas City. "I felt some similarity in spirit" to punk, he recalls. The songs on the album were indeed shorter, harder, and more austere, resembling both country and punk. Even his appearance changed. On the album cover, Bruce looks like a Jersey Shore James Dean, his hands crammed into the pockets of a leather jacket, his hair tousled, resting against Depression-era cabbage rose wallpaper. On the cover of the anthemic punk record Blank Generation, his countenance is nearly as slack as Richard Hell's. The punk rock connection was solidified when Bruce offered Patti Smith a song he couldn't finish via Jimmy Iovine. Her love affair with future husband Fred "Sonic" Smith inspired her to write the poem that completed "Because the Night."

Bruce claims he gave the song away because he was "too cowardly" at the time to create a love ballad. Even in "Born to Run," where he invites a female to go away with him, he is questioning love, and the answer became more elusive as his celebrity grew. The line "I wanna know if love is real" catches the irony of rock celebrity and begins a thread that will run through his albums for years. You start a band not only for the love of music, but for love itself, but once you get there, the intentions of others become suspect. Similarly, success and its ramifications. "I wanna find one face that ain't lookin' through me," he says in "Badlands." Throughout Darkness, Springsteen's inner confusion is obvious.

For years, Bruce had been infusing stories from his early years in Freehold into his onstage pattern, particularly those involving his father, Douglas, and the songs on Darkness are brimming with that melancholy. During concerts, he'd go even deeper, recalling his father's harsh arguments with him. His self-psychoanalysis struck a chord with listeners because he was amusing, and it always led to a fantastic song, and he was doing it to heal, not to offend. Bruce didn't want to be burdened by his father's situation, but he loved him and his family, and he was conscious of his parents' love for each other, which is a very positive thing for any child. Whether consciously or unconsciously, he seemed to understand that working through the past would lead to a better future.

The Darkness tour in 1978-1979 was notoriously combustible, both in terms of performances and the band's emotions. "It was almost like a wave of relief that we'd been able to withstand the pressure," says Weinberg. "There was a ferocity in the band when we finally got out that perhaps wasn't there earlier; it was a take-no-prisoners approach." The stripped-down tracks on the record transferred exceptionally well to the live show, possibly even better in their more dynamic, up-tempo version. The increased intensity, the soul-baring rants, and a front man packed with punk fire who was ripping James Brown moves—it was a show unlike any other. With classic rock on the decline at the time, it was something they craved.

Springsteen began playing larger venues, something he had battled against until the demand for tickets to see him became too overwhelming, but he remained committed to the level of intimacy he shared with his fans. "When I'm onstage," he explains, "I'm almost—I'm half in the audience and half onstage." "And it's really more of a one-on-one situation." Like, I perceive the crowd as a crowd, but also as a one-on-one level."

Though Bruce's star grew, Darkness on the Edge of Town was more of a critical success than a financial success, but it created the groundwork for his first number one album. Some of the songs he'd rejected because they didn't match the mood of Darkness ended up on his next album, The River, released in 1980. Springsteen finally reached number one on Billboard's Top 200 album list eight years after joining Columbia Records. For context, it's worth mentioning that he dethroned Barbra Streisand's Guilty, only to be replaced a month later by Kenny Rogers' Greatest Hits. The status of pop music at the time allowed a major rock artist to accomplish everything except chart-topping success. The River, on the other hand, was Bruce's watershed moment, a huge double disc crammed with radio-ready songs tucked between tempered ballads. Over the next three and a half decades, he'd have 10 more number one records.

During The River sessions, Springsteen became even more prolific, producing "about ninety" songs and leaving behind a treasure trove of unpublished material. He had fought with the thought that the various types of music he was creating were incompatible, only to realize that he could and would embrace them all and yet make a cohesive record. According to him, the album also laid the groundwork for his future undertakings, which will range from low-key records to global rock mega-hits.

The depressing title track was inspired by family. Bruce saw his sister Virginia's troubles after she became pregnant and married her high school sweetheart, and wove them into a cautionary tale: a joyless shotgun wedding, a lonely marriage, insecure job as a laborer, being tortured by lost youth. "Those memories come back to haunt me / They haunt me like a curse / Is a dream a lie if it doesn't come true / Or is it something worse," he sings in "The River." In "Hungry Heart," a song he originally penned for the Ramones, a band that shared his childhood absorption in 1950s and 1960s Top 40 radio, he made another existential crisis sound cheerful.

The River carves a stunning swath through decades of rock, pulling significantly on Bruce's upbringing. The jangle of "The Ties That Bind." The classic quality of "Sherry Darling" and "Out in the Street." The Rolling Stones-inspired "Crush on You." The timeless Americana of "Cadillac Ranch." The Eddie Cochran-inspired song "Ramrod." "Independence Day," another examination of the father-son dynamic in sepia tones.

Despite the wide range of influences packed into a single recording, even a double album, The River is cohesive, thanks in large part to the E Street Band. They were such a tight unit on Born to Run, Darkness on the Edge of Town, and The River that it was difficult to picture Springsteen without them. The complexity of Roy Bittan's piano juxtaposed with Danny Federici's shimmering waves of organ, Steven Van Zandt's mastery of hooks and inimitable harmonies, and Clarence Clemons' distinct saxophone with its clarion cries and lengthy, expressive notes—they all gave Springsteen muscle to match his songwriting and ambition.

Every man in the company was a perfect match. Weinberg fixed a laser-like attention on Bruce throughout performances and had an incredible ability to predict what he'd do next onstage. His and Roy Bittan's orchestra pit experience complemented Bruce's raucous stage theatrics. Van Zandt introduced a garage rock flavor as well as a love of the perfect three-minute pop song. The presence of Clemons and his horn, as well as Federici's glockenspiel, distinguished the ensemble from the rest. "You hear a lot of talk about bands and teams being family," Weinberg explains. "At the time, it was really that, because what we had was our relationships and the music Bruce was writing."

Bruce and the E Street Band were so in sync with one another as they went on The River tour that they had nowhere to go but long. The double record would foreshadow longer sets and three-hour concerts being expanded to four-hour shows. The tour also spanned the globe as they returned to Europe for the first time since Born to Run, laying the groundwork for what would become immense international acclaim.

Springsteen's class consciousness became more political on the River tour. Following the Three Mile Island nuclear disaster, he contributed to the 1979 No Nukes concert at Madison Square Garden in New York City, and by many accounts, was the show's high point, debuting "The River" there. Despite the fact that he did not make a personal anti-nuclear declaration or sign the Musicians United for Safe Energy manifesto, his presence was sufficient. When the tour started, he'd wonder aloud what had become of the American dream. And, the night after Ronald Reagan was elected President in 1980, Bruce reportedly stood onstage at Arizona State University and remarked, "I don't know what you guys think about what happened last night, but I think it's pretty frightening."

Nonetheless, Springsteen ended 1981 on a high note. What should a person with a number one album and the world's best band do next? It would have been no one's guess, not even Bruce's, if he had made a lo-fi recording in his home room and released it as his sixth album.

Chapter 5:
Darkness

"I came home one day and asked my mother if we were Democrats or Republicans," Springsteen recounts of his boyhood. "She said we were Democrats because they stand up for the working class."

Springsteen discovered class consciousness to be instinctual as a baby boomer with a less fortunate, blue-collar upbringing and an inquisitive, anti-authoritarian mind. However, he was cautious to embrace politics in both his profession and his personal life. "I think I voted for McGovern in 1972," Bruce acknowledged a dozen years later when asked if he had ever voted (he had also played a small benefit for the campaign that year in Red Bank, New Jersey). It was something that set him apart from his Columbia labelmate (and fellow John Hammond signee) Bob Dylan, whose writing was rooted in the "broadside" tradition and was unabashedly political. However, the era cannot be ignored. Dylan, who is over a decade older than Bruce, rose to prominence in the 1960s, and his music spoke to a country that was fighting for civil rights and protesting a very unpopular war. Springsteen endured the aftermath of the 1970s as a star, including national disenchantment, war veterans returning to an angry public, and widespread economic distress, all of which influenced his music.

Nonetheless, he was labeled as the "new Dylan" early on, a label that has never actually served anyone's music career well. Like a rodeo bull, Bruce defied the comparison. He was a member of a band, not a solo acoustic act. He had grandiose plans for massive concerts. Dylan preferred Lead Belly and folk music, whilst Bruce preferred Sam and Dave and rhythm 'n' blues. Though they crossed paths at Woody Guthrie, Springsteen was an entertainer first and a provocateur second.

However, following the phenomenal success of The River and the extensive tour that followed, Springsteen went solo acoustic—sort of—releasing Nebraska, an album that was likely close to what Columbia expected when signing him in 1972. The demo-quality home recording was a homogeneous compilation of American noir, dismal tales of shady characters who live and die on the margins. It also served as a link between Springsteen's class consciousness and a broader political knowledge. "Nebraska was about... what happens to people when they're estranged from their friends, community, government, and job," he explains. "Because those are the things that keep you sane, that give some meaning to life."

Greil Marcus considered the album "the most complete and probably the most convincing statement of resistance that Ronald Reagan's U.S.A. has yet elicited," despite the fact that Springsteen used the approach of letting the characters convey parts of his opinions in their voices. If he was going for "apocalyptic grandeur" on Darkness, Nebraska was post-apocalyptic—the sound of a lone driver on a highway to nowhere against a starless sky. The action was daring, intuitive, and counter-intuitive, much like Bruce himself. Despite its somber subject matter and lo-fi sound, it reached the third position on the Billboard Top 200.

Nebraska "kinda came out of nowhere," according to Springsteen. Bruce rented a house on a reservoir in Colts Neck, New Jersey, a posh community of horse farms and golf courses exactly midway between Freehold and Asbury Park but worlds apart from both. He'd penned "Mansion on the Hill" while on tour, and now he'd returned, making real money for the first time in his career, and moved into one, if only briefly. Within a few weeks, he'd written all of the songs that would appear on Nebraska. "I didn't go out much," he continues, "and for some reason, I just started to write." He was also a reader. Springsteen had begun reading books as a young man, due in part to Jon Landau, who introduced him to a number of major American writers and set him on a lifetime literary path. The album Nebraska was heavily influenced by noir novelist Jim Thompson. Howard Zinn's A People's History of the United States, a must-read that tells history from the perspective of the defeated rather than the victorious, broadened the reach of his songs' protagonists. On Darkness on the Edge of Town and Nebraska, Flannery O'Connor's storytelling let him tap into something darker.

O'Connor, according to Springsteen, motivated him to write "kind of smaller than I had been, writing with just detail." He also started recording in smaller sizes. According to longtime Springsteen engineer Toby Scott, Bruce had requested Mike Batlan, the roadie who handled his guitars at the time, to pick up "a little tape machine" and put it up in his spare bedroom. Bruce's objective was to reduce the amount of time he spent in the studio writing, which is an expensive process, by bringing in cassettes of more completely completed songs for the E Street Band to record. By January 1982, Batlan had acquired and installed a Teac TASCAM 144, a Portastudio 4-track, two Shure SM57 microphones, and two mic stands at Springsteen's rented residence.

Nebraska's distinct sound, which was so well suited to the songs that electric versions recorded with the E Street Band were rejected in favor of the original demo, was the product of a technical comedy of errors that they couldn't have duplicated even if they tried. The Portastudio, as simple as it was, was a new machine, and Batlan—a guitar roadie, not a recording engineer—didn't have much time to get to know it. "He got some levels and tried to make sure the meters didn't go into the red too much, and he may have listened briefly with headphones," Scott adds, "but Bruce was eager to get started, so I don't think he got much beyond the basics." In fact, you can hear a touch of distortion as Mike is still finding his levels on some of the early songs they recorded."

Batlan hadn't figured out what the tape speed knob was for, so they recorded everything too quickly and tried to correct it when they mixed the recordings. They were blended down onto Bruce's lone piece of equipment that could connect to the Teac—a filthy old Panasonic boombox. "Bruce had a canoe that he liked to take out on this little branch of the river that flowed near his house, and the previous summer, during one of those trips, the boombox had fallen overboard and sunk in the mud," Scott explains. "When the tide went out later that day, he retrieved it, brought it back to the house, hosed off the mud, and left it on the porch for dead." A week later, he was sitting on the porch reading the Sunday paper when the boom box came back to life.``

They'd also run everything through a Gibson Echoplex, a machine that let them add an echoey "slapback" effect to the tunes before it died. Never mind that neither of them gave much effort to cleaning or aligning the tape heads on any of the equipment they utilized.

Bruce assembled his band in the spring of 1982 to record Nebraska, but ended up recording half of Born in the U.S.A. instead. None of "Electric Nebraska" nailed the mood of the original, despite having the finished demo—the only copy of it—on a cassette in his pocket as a reference. This demo, like the test photos that became the cover of Darkness on the Edge of Town, was what Springsteen published, thanks to adroit studio engineers who were able to adjust for the technological oddities while keeping the integrity of the song.

With Bruce's new composition process and the E Street Band so in sync after years on the road, recording Born in the U.S.A. was a breeze. Though the band recorded between seventy and ninety tracks, depending on who you ask, the majority were completed in just a few takes. According to Max Weinberg, who says he didn't know the song would reprise until Bruce indicated him in the studio, the title track was recorded in two takes. Pandemonium, opacity, Weinberg's booming drum fill, and the band coming back together for a triumphant conclusion can all be heard in the song.

Putting the album together, on the other hand, was a much longer process. Bruce was at another crossroads, and he was struggling to complete Born in the U.S.A. His success was in the rearview mirror, and the future was unknown. Nebraska had removed him from his music family to some level, but he appreciated the independence of it and wondered if that was the way to record in the future. What would it entail for the E Street Band—the guys to whom he'd felt responsible as they all made their way together?

Bruce's depression has returned, stronger than ever. Nebraska sounds gloomy, and for the first time, Bruce couldn't escape it by retreating into what he called his "work life," as he had done in the past. The same hole he depicts in Flannery O'Connor's characters was developing within him. It had driven him to pursue rock 'n' roll glory at the expense of all else, and now that he'd arrived—what next? His loner's pose, which had separated him from people just enough to preserve his focus on composing music, gave him objectivity so that he could turn what he saw into song magic, no longer seemed to suit him. He went on a long cross-country road trip with a friend. "I had a lot of negative feelings," he recalls of the road journey. "I felt empty and floating, as if I'd gotten lost." We eventually arrived in California, where I had a tiny house. And I couldn't sit down when we walked in. I realized that all I wanted to do was get back in the car and go back the other way. And when I returned to New Jersey, I knew I wouldn't want to stay."

"He was feeling suicidal," says music journalist and old friend Dave Marsh. "The despair wasn't particularly shocking. He was on a rocket ride from nothing to something, and now you're getting your ass kissed all hours of the day and night. You may begin to have internal disputes regarding your own self-worth."

"My issues weren't as obvious as drugs," adds Springsteen. "My were different; they were quieter—just as troublesome, but quieter." Because of the undertow of history and self-loathing, there is a great push toward self-obliteration that occurs onstage with all artists. It's both: there's a wonderful discovery of the self as well as a renunciation of the self. For those hours, you are free of yourself; all the voices in your head are gone, just gone..."

Similarly, Johnny Cash, who lived most of his life in anguish and became very ill near the end, remarked that when he walked onstage, he felt fine again, and when he walked offstage, the pain and sickness returned. There were no big rock shows or tours for Bruce to get lost in, but he regularly performed with friends and acquaintances throughout 1982, including the Beaver Brown Band at Big Man West's—Clarence Clemons's nightclub in Red Bank, New Jersey—Dave Edmunds at the Peppermint Lounge in New York City, Stray Cats at the Fast Lane in Asbury Park, and Cats on a Smooth Surface, featuring Bobby Bandiera (who also played for Bruce). He performed at wedding banquets for Southside Johnny and, later, Steven Van Zandt (to Maureen Santoro, his real-life and fictional bride). In March, he and Roy Bittan traveled to Los Angeles to record a song for Donna Summer with the musician and producer

Quincy Jones. He performed alongside Jackson Browne at the Rally for Disarmament in Central Park in June. That November, he paid a visit to his engineers Chuck Plotkin and Toby Scott when they were working on a session with Bette Midler; as is his custom, he gave her "Pink Cadillac." When "Dancing in the Dark" was released as a single, it became a B-side.

Songs were being rejected as Springsteen, Van Zandt, Landau, Plotkin, and Scott pieced together Born in the U.S.A. from multiple sessions. Bruce had composed between seventy and ninety songs (depending on who you ask) and was rejecting those that his team thought would be hits, such as "I'm on Fire," "I'm Goin' Down," "Cover Me," and "Pink Cadillac." According to Marsh, Bruce approached E Street Band members for their thoughts for the first time. The arduous, painstaking process of putting the album together took nearly two years, during which time Bruce wrestled with the idea of who he wanted to be, what he wanted out of fame, what he would give back, and how he would remain true to his core beliefs if this next effort made him the global superstar that his record label had predicted. Near the conclusion, an irritated Springsteen was pressed by Landau to write a single, which he thought was still lacking. Bruce returned to his hotel room and wrote "Dancing in the Dark" in one night. "It was as if my heart spoke directly through my mouth, without even passing through my brain," he says. "The chorus just poured out of me."

Springsteen won his first Grammy for the song (for Best Male Rock Vocal Performance). Its video, produced by Brian De Palma and including an appearance by pre-Friends Courteney Cox, catapulted him to MTV stardom. Again, Bruce flawlessly expressed his irritation and perplexity at that time in his life, as well as the psychology behind it, beneath the joyful music. "Look, you cannot underestimate the fine power of self-loathing in all of this," he says. "You think, I don't like anything I'm seeing or doing, but I have to change myself, I have to transform myself." I don't know a single artist who doesn't rely on it. Nobody would be fucking doing it if you were incredibly satisfied with yourself! ... That notion of 'I need to reinvent myself, my town, my audience'—the yearning for renewal—is a motive."

The title tune served a similar purpose via an even more inventive narrative style. After reading Ron Kovic's Born on the Fourth of July, Bruce had come to understand the plight of the men who had gone to Vietnam and fought the war he had dodged. "Born in the U.S.A." is a powerful and touching tribute to them, but it also mines Springsteen's tale, that of a guy at a crossroads, attempting to cope with his new circumstances. His ability to acknowledge the individuals he writes about while pulling from his own emotional well for depth and potentially catharsis is one of his greatest abilities as a songwriter. Those two songs elevated that ability to a new level.

Born in the U.S.A. commands attention from the first notes. Its synth sounds and pop leanings were quintessentially '80s; it was published in June 1984. The album was meant to elevate Bruce from rock star to icon, and it succeeded, selling 15 million copies in the United States and 30 million globally. Only Michael Jackson and Janet Jackson have had as many Billboard Hot 100 Top 10 singles from a single album—"Dancing in the Dark," "Cover Me," "Born in the U.S.A.," "My Hometown," "I'm on Fire," "Glory Days," and "I'm Goin' Down"—and seven of them made the Top 10. Most notably, underlying the grandeur and dazzling melodies that drew millions of new listeners were the emotional stories that kept his early followers returning. All of his hard work, worry, and soul-searching had paid off for him, not only professionally, but also deeply personally. Despite his reservations, Springsteen was able to reach unprecedented popularity while remaining true to himself.

The flag-draped cover, shot by famed photographer Annie Leibovitz, featured Springsteen's much-touted blue-jeaned butt, toned from running and weight training—a fitness regimen he'd begun and kept up over the years. Bruce didn't make much of it, except to vehemently refute reports that it was a picture of him peeing on the flag, despite the fact that he'd allegedly wanted his face on the cover because it wasn't on Nebraska. "We took a lot of different types of pictures," he explains, "and in the end, the picture of my ass looked better than the picture of my face, so that's what went on the cover."

Given the album's red-white-and-blue design, the fact that 1984 was an election year—the year in which George Orwell's futuristic novel of an oppressive government was set—and the title track's let-freedom-ring tone, it's no surprise that Born in the U.S.A. was co-opted by politicians. Following a Springsteen concert, conservative writer George Will penned "A Yankee Doodle Springsteen," ignoring the protest components of Bruce's songs in favor of his rugged individualism flecked with glimmers of hope. A week later, President Ronald Reagan mentioned Bruce in an addendum to his stump speech in Hammonton, New Jersey, the Pine Barrens town known as the world's blueberry capital: "America's future rests in a thousand dreams inside your hearts; it rests in the message of hope in songs so many young Americans admire: New Jersey's own Bruce Springsteen." And this work is all about assisting you in making your aspirations come true."

Conservatives misinterpreted "Born in the USA" for jingoism, as the New Jersey State Assembly did when it named "Born to Run," a song about leaving the state, its "unofficial youth anthem." Requests to utilize the song, likely from campaign operatives who hadn't listened beyond the rousing chorus, were denied. Though Springsteen was still a long way from full political involvement, he wasn't about to let his music be used for evil. "When Reagan mentioned my name in New Jersey, I felt it was another manipulation, and I felt I had to disassociate myself from the president's kind words," he adds.

If they had listened to the lyrics of "Born in the U.S.A.," they would have heard the story of a Vietnam warrior who returned to a country that no longer needed him. They would have heard an even more horrifying story of a soldier's return if they had turned over the 45 rpm single and played its B-side, "Shut Out the Light," inspired by Ron Kovic's novel. Springsteen has long questioned the injustice of who fights wars for the United States. When his conscription number came up in the late 1960s, he wondered why his life was worth less than a rich boy who could defer because his parents had money or political weight. Boys from Freehold he knew served and died, notably Castiles drummer Bart Haynes, who left an indelible impression on Springsteen. In the early 1980s, he contacted Kovic and Bob Muller, both injured veterans, peace activists, and veterans' advocates. Bruce agreed to make an upcoming concert a fundraiser for Muller's ailing organization, Vietnam Veterans of America, for which he raised over a quarter-million dollars.

Politicians wanted Springsteen, but he refused at the time, even when Walter Mondale's campaign asked for his assistance in opposing Reagan in 1984. Bruce declined to say if he thought Mondale was a better candidate. "I don't know," he admitted. "I believe there are significant differences, but I'm not sure how significant they are." And pre-election rhetoric makes it tough to determine. It always seems to change when they suddenly walk in. That's why I don't have a strong attachment to electoral politics right now—it can't be the greatest approach to identify the best man for the most difficult job. I'd like to try to work more directly with people; to find a method for my band to connect with the areas we visit. That, I suppose, is a political activity, a method to avoid the whole electoral process. Politics in human beings. I believe that individuals can do a great deal on their own. That's what I'm trying to figure out right now: Where do the aesthetic issues you write about intersect with physical action, direct involvement in the communities from which your audience comes? It appears to be an unavoidable evolution of what our band has been doing, of the concept for which we got into this. We wanted to play because we wanted to meet females, make a lot of money, and make a small difference in the world, you know?" Bruce's "human" political activism was incorporated into his tours. In addition to raising funds for veterans, he began assisting local food banks and environmental groups in promoting awareness and collecting funds at his performances, which was no minor feat given his huge popularity. Forget about selling out arenas; he could sell out many nights at a single venue. He made his debut in August 1985 at Giants Stadium in East Rutherford, New Jersey, with a six-night run. Regardless of how enormous the shows got, Bruce managed the seemingly impossible feat of making tens of thousands of people feel connected to him and to one another.

Chapter 6:
Second Skin

On "I Wanna Marry You," from The River, Bruce Springsteen watches a single mother walking around the neighborhood with her children and fantasizes about having a relationship with her. He approaches the issue of love in the same way he approaches all other aspects of working-class life: with a gloomy pragmatism and an occasional sliver of hope.

Prior to The River, Bruce, as he admits, was not a huge fan of penning love songs. He was also not big on relationships, despite the fact that he had girlfriends and claimed to have lived with one for around two years in his early twenties. "I can't have any women," he confided to acquaintances early in his career. "I have to give my music everything I have." Though true—it would have been impossible for him to reach his unique niche in rock music without complete dedication—such declarations no longer made sense to him after two decades of doing it.

Springsteen had just purchased his first real home, another "mansion on the hill," in Rumson, New Jersey. He'd wished for a home for the automobiles he'd accumulated over the years, including the 1960 Corvette he'd purchased with his Born to Run money, which had been parked at various friends' homes. After the Born in the U.S.A. tour, he built the home studio he'd always wanted so he wouldn't have to drive to New York every time he wanted to record. After a lifetime of renting, couch surfing, and sleeping on the beach or at Tinker West's surfboard factory, buying a house in his home state was a small step toward settling down. Constant traveling had been an important part of expanding his fan base, but as long as he was on the road, he didn't have to settle down or evaluate his emotional life in any way other than songwriting. He describes the three- and four-hour presentations as "born out of pure fear, self-loathing, and self-hatred." "That's why my performances were so long. They weren't long because I had a preconceived notion or plan that they should be. I couldn't stop until I was completely exhausted. "Extremely charred."

He began talk therapy after falling into a deep despair around the time of Nebraska, which he would continue for three decades. "Finding some stuff out, then running away," he recalls, was the initial procedure. Springsteen's emotional intelligence had matured to the point where he understood he needed guidance if he wanted to open himself to others. He didn't want the "unfulfilled life" of the father character in "I Wanna Marry You." Jon Landau referred to him as "the smartest person I've ever known—not the most informed or educated, but the smartest." If you ever find yourself in a situation—a practical matter or an artistic quandary—his reading of the persons involved is superb. He's far ahead." He'd have to read himself now.

Patti Scialfa, Bruce's wife since 1991 and the first full-time female E Street Band member (Suki Lahav had joined temporarily in the mid-1970s), said it best. "When you are that serious, that creative, and that non-trusting on an intimate level, and your art has given you so much, your ability to create something becomes your medicine," she adds. "It's the only thing that has given you stability, joy, and self-esteem." So you're thinking, 'This part of me, no one is going to touch.' That works while you're young because it gets you from point A to point B. It doesn't work when you get older and try to start a family and have children. I believe that some artists are so good at protecting the well from which they draw their inspiration that they are essentially protecting malignant elements of themselves. You see that something is broken. It's not simply that you're the mythical lone wolf; something is broken. Bruce is quite intelligent. He wanted a family, he wanted a relationship, and he worked as hard as he works on his music."

Theoretically, someone with such unwavering drive may apply it to more than one aspect of their life. In practice, though, it is not that straightforward. Bruce had one thing going for him: family. The same family whose difficulties inspired his every triumph may push him to move beyond his solitary identity and into a serious adult relationship. His parents remained married until his father died of cancer in 1998, at the age of 73. Virginia, whose teen pregnancy/marriage he'd memorialized in "The River," had blissfully remained with her high school love. Even if Bruce lacked the emotional abilities to carry his personal life forward, he had some encouraging examples. Trying to bridge the distance he'd created between his family and himself was part of his own development.

But, in 1984, he was still struggling with the issue of his single status. "I'm not sure if I'm a huge family man. My family has been my backing band. "I've always been like that," he explained at the time. "I think I did it on purpose when I was younger, because I knew I only had sixty dollars that month, and I had to live on that sixty dollars, and I couldn't get married or involved at the time." And then it simply became a way of life for me. It truly became a way of life for me... I'm just not interested in getting married right now. I've committed to doing my job right now, and that's essentially what I do. Someday, I'd like to have the full package—wife and kids."

He gave it a chance five and a half months later. He married actress and former model Julianne Phillips after a brief engagement. It was May 13, 1985, at the height of Bruce's rock career; he'd just returned from the Born in the U.S.A. tour's Australia/Japan leg. She'd followed him to Japan, and then to Lake Oswego, Oregon, where she was raised and her parents still lived. When helicopters descended on the event two days later, Bruce reportedly said, "I do not believe or comprehend the world that I live in." Almost two weeks later, Bruce and the E Street Band were back in New Jersey, recording the video for "Glory Days" at the famed rock club Maxwell's in Hoboken with local John Sayles directing. Little Steven Van Zandt and Phillips both made appearances. When the tour ended in October of that year at the Los Angeles Memorial Coliseum, Bruce brought his new bride onstage during "Dancing in the Dark," rather than his usual ritual of picking a girl from the audience, in front of an audience of 85,000. "I'd like to thank all of my fans for coming out here," he stated as the night came to a close. "This has been the most incredible year of my life." "I feel like the luckiest man on the planet."

They were shot together at the Rock and Roll Hall of Fame induction ceremony at the Waldorf Astoria in New York City in January 1988. Bruce inducted Bob Dylan, dressed in a silvery jacket, collared white shirt, and bolo tie, and credited him with broadening the concept of rock artistry and the pop song itself. "Bob freed your mind in the same way that Elvis freed your body," he explained.

He and Phillips split the next year after publicly separating for a few months. Neither has said much about their three-year marriage or how it ended, but Bruce has admitted to some of the issues he was dealing with at the time. "The emotions of mine that were uncovered by trying to have an adult life with a partner and make that work uncovered a lot of things I'd avoided and tried not to deal with previously," he adds.

His 1987 album Tunnel of Love delves into these ideas, with the title alluding to how the promise of new love gives way to a lack of clarity as the record develops. The album fits into the arc of his career like a puzzle piece, expounding on issues he'd addressed a decade earlier—a grown-up protagonist who wants to commit but isn't sure he's ready to trust, who still doubts love and is troubled by uncertainty. The songs were more mature, polished, and contemplative, a natural progression following the blockbuster Born in the USA. Whether Bruce avoided penning love songs in the 1970s, he made up for it today with first-person stories that felt as lonely and confused as he did when he wanted to know "if love is real" at the age of twenty-four. Also, he'd never felt completely at ease with the image of himself that had given him a global celebrity earlier in the decade. "I thought I had to reintroduce myself as a songwriter, in a very non-iconic role," he says of the record. "And it was a welcome relief."

The tour was just as different as prior tours. It was shorter in duration (named "Tunnel of Love Express," it only lasted about five months) and performed in smaller settings. Around a thousand people packed the Worcester Centrum on opening night, including Rob Lowe and Boston Celtics forward Kevin McHale, to see Bruce and the E Street Band's first official concert in two and a half years. Fans without seats outside the arena offered $500 or more for last-minute tickets, but nearly none were sold.

The performances were staged theatrically, with the band rehearsing for around six weeks at Bruce's local hangout, the Expo Theater at the now-defunct Fort Monmouth army base. Onstage, a carnival theme was built as a play on the album's title tune, complete with a barker, ticket booth, fun house, and sideshow banners symbolizing heaven and hell, each with a Bruce-faced devil. The artists had to purchase fun house tickets in order to make their entrance. Even the song selection was noticeably altered, with some crowd-pleasers deleted and "Born to Run" performed in a calmer acoustic style, with Bruce adding that he was no longer "running."

The shows began with the title track from his new album and were separated into two segments, one filled with new material and tinged with melancholy and the other with old favorites. The other was more energetic, making good use of Bruce's horn section, which included Richie "LaBamba" Rosenberg (who'd later become known as a member of the Max Weinberg 7 on Late Night with Conan O'Brien).

Bruce had repositioned the band to "mix things up," putting backup vocalist Patti Scialfa to his side, where Clarence Clemons had stood. He required a female counterpart to express these songs and themes, mournful in the first set and waggish in the second. On "You Can Look but You Better Not Touch," Bruce and the band flirted with Scialfa.

Following the conclusion of the Tunnel of Love Express tour, the band embarked on the six-week, twenty-date Human Rights Now! international tour in support of Amnesty International. The concerts were dedicated to promoting awareness of the Universal Declaration of Human Rights' fortieth anniversary, and included Bruce and the E Street Band on the road alongside Sting, Peter Gabriel, Tracy Chapman, Youssou N'Dour, and musicians from each country they visited. When the tour stopped in Oakland, California, Roy Orbison, whom Springsteen had inducted into the Rock and Roll Hall of Fame the year before (and who would pass away just a few months later), made a cameo appearance. Traveling together with few luxuries across Costa Rica, India, Zimbabwe, and the Ivory Coast, the musicians built incredible on and off stage camaraderie. Nils Lofgren of E Street says he played basketball with Branford Marsalis and that Roy Bittan beat practically everyone at Ping-Pong. Sting sang with

Bruce on "The River," and Bruce sang "Every Breath You Take" with him in return. Fans who noticed Springsteen mingling with other artists and speculated that he would be ready for a new project were correct.

Springsteen began to distance himself from his music family as he considered having his own family. Tunnel of Love not only reflects his personal life, but also his departure from the E Street Band. They merely played on parts of it, with drum machines and synthesizers filling in the gaps. The tour to promote it and Human Rights Now! would be their final performance for a decade. Springsteen made the arduous phone calls to each member in 1989, with different degrees of success. Clemons was enraged, but Weinberg says he wasn't surprised; the warning flags had been there for a long time. "We stopped playing together for ten years," Bruce explains, "partially because I ran out of ideas for where to take the band next, but I also think people were a little tired of each other." That was just something that happened." There had been talk since Nebraska's solo attempt, but after the Born in the U.S.A. tour took them all to another level, it may have surprised some. Who would disband the best rock band ever? "He had been doing one thing for a long time, and he wanted to try something new," Van Zandt explained. "I don't think it gets much more dramatic than that."

In the year that followed, he only had a few gigs, practically none of which were his. Bruce frequented small clubs along the Jersey Shore with buddies including Bobby Bandiera and Gary US Bonds. He performed with Jimmy Cliff and Ringo Starr's All-Starr Band, which now included Nils Lofgren and Clarence Clemons. He opened for Max Weinberg's band Killer Joe at the Stone Pony before performing at Roy Bittan's wedding. He also performed at a few West Coast locations. He went on a trip. He was riding his motorcycle.

Bruce boarded a silver and blue Harley-Davidson and set out for the Grand Canyon (or so others would later report), accompanied by four bodyguards—three on bikes and one in a vehicle. They arrived in Prescott, Arizona, and proceeded to Whiskey Row, stopping for Cokes at the historic Palace Bar and then at Matt's Saloon, a honky-tonk refuge for bikers and country music enthusiasts. Waylon

Jennings, Buck Owens, and Lee Hazlewood were all regulars at Matt's in the 1960s. While working in the region, Steve McQueen and Sam Peckinpah had hung around there. Bruce strolled in for a few afternoon beers, but before long he was up onstage with the Mile High Band, a group of local musicians. The crowd rose from fewer than ten to more than a hundred as they worked their way through an hour of classic, eminently jammable favorites including Elvis Presley's "Don't Be Cruel," Chuck Berry's "Sweet Little Sixteen," and "Route 66," and a lone Springsteen original ("I'm on Fire"). When admirers surrounded Bruce, he leapt over the bar and posed for pictures with tattooed, Harley-gear-clad bartender/biker Brenda "Bubbles" Pechanec before sprinting across the street, jumping back on the bike, and speeding down Montezuma Street. Bubbles had just married for the ninth time in a motorcycle wedding ceremony officiated by a priest known as "Catfish." She had also racked up six-figure medical expenditures after battling cancer the previous year. Bruce eventually paid off her loan.

Springsteen admits he was in a sad place after the Tunnel of Love and was difficult to be around while he formed his connection with Patti Scialfa. "She had a very keen eye for all of my nonsense," he recalls. "She was aware of it. She was able to confront me about it. I'd honed my skills as a master manipulator. 'Oh, I'm leaving the house for a little bit, and I'm heading down...' "I've always had a way of moving off, away, back, and creating distance." Scialfa also realized that he was depressed—she'd experienced it herself—and knew how to deal with him. "I felt very much like akin to him," she recalls.

There was a strong bond between the two. Scialfa had created a career out of music, from penning songs as a teenager to traveling with Southside Johnny to singing on the Rolling Stones' Dirty Work album. She was also from the Jersey Shore. She grew up in Deal, which was a little more affluent than Bruce's blue-collar birthplace, but she came to Asbury Park for fun and music. Friends recall her as the stereotypical rock chick, driving around town in a muscle vehicle with the radio blasting. She'd even called Springsteen once, in response to an ad in the Asbury Park Press for a singer for a "touring band, must be able to travel." He gently advised that she stay in school because she was fifteen.

Scialfa accomplished just that, enrolling as the sole woman in her class at the University of Miami's famous jazz institution, the Frost School of Music. She sent demos to record labels and had interest from Jerry Wexler at Atlantic, who had wooed Aretha Franklin away from Columbia and worked with a slew of other music legends. Scialfa returned to Manhattan to finish her studies at New York University, where she received a music degree. She waitressed and busked on the street with pals (future E Street partners Soozie Tyrell and Lisa Lowell) while living in the city, sometimes dressing up in cocktail clothes for effect.

Scialfa was a rock chick, a girl who could hang with the boys, yet she was and still is graceful, almost matriarchal. Those attributes were still visible when she was inducted into the Rock and Roll Hall of Fame with the rest of the E Street Band in 2014, as she honored her three children and husband. If Bruce was going to have the family he desired, it appears he couldn't have found a better match.

He and Patti lived in New York City for a while, but he didn't enjoy city life. So they moved west, just like his parents had done two decades before, but with far more money, settling into a $13 million property in Beverly Hills. "People have always come west to re-discover or re-create themselves in some way," he explains. "This is the town of re-creation, mostly distorted, but the raw material is here; it's just what you make of it." I enjoy the geography and the desert, and a half-hour drive from my house takes you to the San Gabriel Mountains, where there are a hundred miles and only one store. It was just a nice place to start over, for Patti and myself to discover each other, ourselves, and have our children." Evan James Springsteen was born in 1990, with Jessica following in 1991 and Sam following in 1994.

Babies and devotion sparked a different kind of artistic motivation. Human Touch, Bruce's tenth album, took nearly two years to complete, yet he admits it still seemed unfinished at the time. "It was nine months after my [first] son was born," he explains. "I was a father, and I had a genuine relationship with Patti, which had eluded me for a long time." He experienced a rush of creativity just before he and Scialfa married, creating the songs that would become his ninth album, Lucky Town. "I wrote and recorded the whole thing in about three weeks," he explains. "It's just one of those records that just comes pouring out of you, and they always tend to be more direct."

Human Touch and Lucky Town were both released in the spring of 1992. "I realized that the two albums together kind of tell one story," Bruce explains. "There's Tunnel of Love, what happened in between, which is Human Touch, and Lucky Town." 'Well, hey—Guns N' Roses!' I exclaimed. They released two albums; maybe I'll give it a shot."

Human Touch has a blues and soul flavor to it, which is accentuated by vocal performances from Sam Moore of Sam and Dave and Bobby Hatfield of the Righteous Brothers. Bruce enlisted the help of Roy Bittan, who had collaborated with him on the song cycle, and founding E Streeter David Sancious. Human Touch was recorded at several professional Los Angeles studios, and Springsteen hired session musicians such as future American Idol judge Randy Jackson on bass and Toto drummer Jeff Porcaro, who'd played with Toto and left his mark on thousands of recording sessions (and who died just a few months before the albums were released). As a result, it has a late 1980s/early 1990s sound, and tracks like "57 Channels (And Nothin' On)" are deliciously anachronistic. "Pony Boy," the album's acoustic ending track, is an outlier. It segues perfectly into the earthier, more twangy Lucky Town, which is based on a song Springsteen's grandmother sang to him and he sang to his first son. Bruce played the majority of the instruments on the song, which was mostly recorded in his California home. Though the lyrics are heavily influenced by his newly acquired status as a family man, he still seems as though he's coming to grips with his accomplishment. "I've struggled with a lot of things in the last two, three years, and it's been extremely rewarding." I've been extremely happy, the happiest I've ever been in my entire life. And it isn't the one-dimensional concept of 'happy.' Accepting a great deal of death, misery, and mortality. It's throwing away the screenplay and letting the chips fall where they may."

Chapter 7:
Lost Years

Springsteen himself refers to the 1990s as his "lost years" in terms of his professional life, despite the fact that he received two of the highest distinctions in entertainment during that time—induction into the Rock and Roll Hall of Fame and an Oscar—and his followers remained devoted. They nevertheless camped out for days to secure concert tickets, despite the fact that it was a different show with a different band—the "Other Band," as some dubbed them, with five backup vocalists and just E Street keyboardist Roy Bittan remaining. Springsteen fans snapped up 200,000 tickets in two and a half hours for an eleven-show run at the Meadowlands venue in his home state of New Jersey. Bruce's songwriting remained as strong as ever, and his albums sold millions of copies, but they didn't last as long on the charts as they had previously. Critics argued his success had made him appear "out of touch," and he responded brilliantly. "I kept my promises," he declares. "I didn't get tired of it. I didn't squander my time. I did not perish. "I didn't abandon my musical values."

The song "Streets of Philadelphia" earned him an Oscar, four more Grammys, and increased global renown when it climbed even higher abroad. Springsteen wrote it at the request of filmmaker Jonathan Demme, who was working on the film Philadelphia at the time.

Demme, who got his start in film working with B-movie great Roger Corman, was fresh off the huge success of The Silence of the Lambs, which had swept the top five Oscar categories. Demme used his momentum to tackle the issue of HIV and AIDS in the picture about a lawyer (Tom Hanks) who loses his job after contracting the illness. The sickness was still a source of enormous fear and discrimination at the time. Demme had no intention of making the picture for people who already knew about or were living with HIV and AIDS. He wanted to start a national conversation, and using the music was a perfect method to do so. He'd asked Neil Young to write a song for the film as a huge rock introduction. Young had emerged as a godfather of grunge in the early 1990s, playing loud, discordant music with Sonic Youth, Pearl Jam, and Soundgarden. He turned to

Springsteen when Young provided him with a softer, more introspective song (which he used to finish the film). "Streets of Philadelphia" was written in two days by Bruce and is a calm, atmospheric rock ballad driven by synthesizers and drum machines. It reflected not only Bruce's musical principles, but also his moral compass. The emotion he injects into a man's fight for life demonstrates his own astounding compassion, especially at a time when many people did not want to hear about AIDS.

Springsteen speaks for the song's ravaged protagonist as he walks from the city's shining towers and symbol of American freedom—the Liberty Bell—through neighborhoods blighted by crack consumption (a wall with "Don't Believe the Pipe" spray-painted on it serves as a reminder of that particular epidemic) and poverty, exiting as a small group of men gather around a trash can fire, set against a glittering skyline. After filming the video, Bruce was so affected that he contributed $45,000 to one of its venues, Sacks Playground on Fourth and Washington Streets in South Philly. "Springsteen was very, very nice," says Ron Petrofsky, district manager for the city's leisure department. "He said he saw the work the community and playground volunteers were doing and wanted to help." We could certainly benefit from it." The playground, which has over four acres of recreational space, is still operational today.

Springsteen's ability to depict a character's life and tribulations was moving. The video's imagery of firefighters, schoolchildren, and ruined neighborhoods set against a backdrop of skyscrapers emphasized Bruce's growing class consciousness. It was also a fitting metaphor for the toll HIV and AIDS had taken on its victims, as well as the sluggish response Americans had as a nation to it. Bruce highlighted the importance of music as a tool for change when he stood up to accept his Oscar for Best Original Song at the 66th Academy Awards ceremony. "I have to share this with you, Neil [Young]," he added. "You do your best work, hoping that it brings out the best in your audience and that some of it seeps into the real world and people's everyday lives." And it takes the sting out of fear by allowing us to acknowledge one other through our differences. That was always one of the things I believed popular art was meant to be about, along with commercialization and all that other nonsense. I just wanted to thank you, Jonathan, for including me in your picture; I'm delighted my song contributed to its concepts and acceptance."

With "Streets of Philadelphia," Springsteen moved a step closer to officially aligning himself with social and political problems. The song made him more conscious of LGBT concerns. He appeared on a VH1 special with Melissa Etheridge in 1995—he was an influence on her music, and she'd lost a Grammy to him for "Streets of Philadelphia"—and they became friends. "I think the experience of having his song in Philadelphia led him to meet a lot of gay people and learn a lot about our lives," she told the New York Times in 1996. "When we go to his house, my girlfriend Julie [Cypher] is always with me, and he always treats us as a couple." I've often expressed my anger about not being able to legally marry, and he is always supportive and empathetic."

Springsteen's conscience had always played a role in his career, as he had aided veterans' groups, environmental causes, food banks, and other charity organizations. Nonetheless, as he progressed from creating songs rooted in class consciousness to increased political awareness and, eventually, campaigned for John Kerry and Barack Obama, his audience changed with him. Even if they didn't agree with his politics—which many did and still do—Bruce's unwavering support for the underdog was something that anybody could get behind. The fact that he invested his own money in what he was promoting not only helped the world, but it also gave him credibility among both believers and those who were only interested in the rock.

Bruce's increased political awareness served as the foundation for his next production, The Ghost of Tom Joad, which he recorded at his Los Angeles home studio. With his previous three albums, he had delved deeply into his inner life, and "Streets of Philadelphia" reminded him that the world outside himself still demanded his attention. Since the late 1970s, Springsteen had been a fan of Oscar-winning filmmaker John Ford's version of The Grapes of Wrath, and later, the novel by John Steinbeck. Now he saw a comparison between the struggle of its protagonist, Tom Joad, and what he viewed as an assault on President Lyndon Johnson's Great Society.

These programs aided in the formation of the middle class and the support of lower-income households. They had also shaped his parents' and his own political ideologies.

During his tenure in his little Hollywood Hills house in the mid-1980s, Bruce also predicted the burgeoning Latino population. He examined the immigrant experience on a personal level as he witnessed it play out in California, how people arrived, how they were treated, what they came for, and what they got, as the granddaughter of an Italian immigrant—his maternal grandmother—who lived to 102 and never learned to speak English. "If you go to my hometown, Freehold, there's a tremendous Hispanic influence, and that was California fifteen years ago," he explains. "So, when I wrote The Ghost of Tom Joad and wrote a lot about what was going on, it felt like, 'This is what the country's going to look like in another ten or fifteen years.'" All of the immigration concerns that people are trying to avoid right now... were all in the headlines and in your face in California in the early 1990s."

Ghost, like the acoustic, home-recorded Nebraska, has an even stronger sense of desperation. The album's title tune begins with a man sitting by a fire, waiting for the ghost of Tom Joad, with the growing realization that atonement will not come. Ex-convicts discover that striving to live a normal life is futile ("Straight Time"). "Sinaloa Cowboys" cross the Mexican border into the United States to gather fruit for slave pay, only to die in a meth lab. In San Diego, "border boys" prostitute themselves to clients in flashy cars ("Balboa Park"). Bruce won a Grammy for Best Contemporary Folk Album for the album.

In November 1995, Bruce embarked on a solo acoustic tour of small venues in support of Ghost. On opening night at the Count Basie Theater in Red Bank, New Jersey, he urged the audience of about 1500 people to remain silent. "Thank you very much," he expressed gratitude. "All right, before we go any further... a few ground rules (laughs)... One is, umm... All kidding aside, I wrote a lot of this music tonight, and part of the composition is the silence in between the spaces, so I really need your help in, um, keeping the silence during the songs." He'd start each program with a shortened version of the disclaimer, usually with a joke. "Any singing or clapping will result in the arrest of a special contingent of New Jersey state police, uh..." If you have any of those little cameras, please keep them in your pocket or crush 'em under your left foot or something, and it is a community event, so if someone is making too much noise around you, feel free to advise them to please shut the fuck up in the most constructive way possible, all right... uh … Now that I've gotten that off my chest (chuckles),... Thank you for your assistance."

The tour spanned a year and a half, with Bruce taking summer and winter holidays to spend time with his family. After a year, he returned to his hometown of Freehold and performed at his Catholic school's 1,300-seat gymnasium, St. Rose of Lima. He hadn't been there in about three decades with the Castiles. Marion Vinyard (Tex's wife) was in the crowd, and he dedicated "This Hard Land" to her, as was Maria Espinoza Ayala, the recipient of Bruce's first kiss, whom he thanked from the stage. He performed the event as a fundraiser for the church's community hall, which served the burgeoning Hispanic population, with the condition that the $30 tickets be sold solely to borough residents.

Bruce had spent part of 1995 with the E Street Band to promote his Greatest Hits album, but near the close of the decade he decided to reassemble everyone for a full-fledged tour. Rehearsals began on a few frigid March days in 1999 at Asbury Park's Convention Hall, a Renaissance-style monument towering up from the beachfront and looming over the beach. Fans gathered outside to listen, exchanging information online, attempting to piece together what was going on and which songs would be featured on the reunion tour that would take them from April 1999 to the new century.

Springsteen was honored into the Rock and Roll Hall of Fame while rehearsing with old pals. Members of the E Street Band were not recognized. It would be more than a decade and a half before the complete band arrived, and on the night they did, Bruce shared a story about the argument that ensued. "I stood in my darkened kitchen with Steve Van Zandt sixteen years ago, a few days before my own induction," he added. "Steve had just returned to the band after a fifteen-year hiatus, and he was petitioning me to get us all inducted into the Hall of Fame together." I paid attention, because the Hall of Fame had its own set of regulations, and I was proud of my independence. We hadn't played together in ten years, we were estranged, and we were just getting started on re-forming. We had no idea what the future held. And possibly the ghosts of some ancient grudges played a role. It was a conundrum because we've never been quite fish or fowl. And Steve was quiet but tenacious. And at the end of our chat, he simply stated, "Yeah, I understand." But the legend is Bruce Springsteen and the E Street Band."

Chapter 8:
The Rising

Nick Hornby, an English novelist and longtime Springsteen fan, included a reference to Bruce in his 1995 novel High Fidelity. His protagonist, Rob Fleming, muses on the song "Bobby Jean," in which a man seeks an old flame, which Rob examines. In the film, John Cusack, who plays the Americanized Rob Gordon, conjures up Bruce. Rob sits alone on his bed, contemplating contacting his "top five" ex-girlfriends to try to figure out where the relationships went wrong, and has an imaginary conversation with Springsteen.

Bruce casually plays on the blues, encouraging Rob to follow in the footsteps of the character in "Bobby Jean," Telecaster in his lap, Fender Twin behind him. "That's what you're looking for, to get ready to start over, and it'd be beneficial to you." "Good luck and goodbye to your all-time top five," he says, referring to the lyrics of his song. Springsteen appeared to be a father figure, or at the very least a big brother, imparting wisdom and clarity in the midst of chaos.

When the film was released in 2000, Bruce was on the rise following a period of relative quiet. The reunion tour was on the road not to promote any one album, but to offer a rolling rock 'n' roll resurrection to fans in a year when 'N SYNC, Eminem, and Britney Spears were the top-selling musicians. Grunge had passed. 'N SYNC sold 2.4 million copies of No Strings Attached in its first week, just overlapping the rise of Napster, which would upend the paradigm that allowed musicians to achieve such high levels of album sales. It was a bleak moment for rock music, and by March of 2000, it was a bleak time to be born in the United States of America, with a stock market crisis and mass layoffs sweeping the country.

Springsteen gave what rock fans wanted at the time, whether it was his great sense for recognizing cultural moments, his instinct to deviate from music industry trends, or simply a yearning to rock again. His onstage pattern became an outpouring of the life-affirming salvation that rock 'n' roll could provide as he played the preacher. His face fills with excitement as he dances and shuffles his way around the stage, guitar slung across his back, Steven Van Zandt casting pleased and knowing glances. Bruce appears to be overjoyed to be making songs with his old band.

That motivation and healing would be important in 2001, just after 9/11, as Americans dealt with the first attack on their homeland since Pearl Harbor. Following The Ghost of Tom Joad, which put him in the center of loss, Bruce moved his family back to New Jersey, just a few minutes from where he was raised, in the mid-1990s. More than 700 people died in the attacks in New Jersey, second only to New York, with 147 of them from his home county of Monmouth. During the chaotic days following the assaults, a Rumson resident named Edwin Sutphin spotted Bruce driving his vintage Corvette in a Sea Bright parking lot. Sutphin claims he pulled down his window, locked eyes with Bruce, and exclaimed, "We need you now!" as loudly as he could.

Springsteen, who made few public appearances in 2001, would keep a low profile until 10 days after the assault. He opened America: A Tribute to Heroes, the national telethon held in three cities, with an acoustic guitar, harmonica, and a few E Street Band members, transforming "My City of Ruins," a rumination on Asbury Park's capricious fortunes, into part of a song cycle that would help heal a wounded nation. Sitting in the seat of grief, he performed at a series of benefit concerts for victims' families, including one organized by Garry Tallent in Red Bank.

He'd started writing several of the songs for The Rising in the late 1990s, but the songs took on new meaning in the aftermath of the attacks. Springsteen's father died in 1998, and some of the songs were tinged with a sense of loss that translated to the grief that people everywhere were experiencing.

But, when he entered the studio for the first time since Born in the USA to record a full E Street Band album, coaxing a studio sound that satisfied Bruce after a year and a half on the road proved difficult. Springsteen claims to have lost his "rock voice." He'd find it with Brendan O'Brien, who'd worked with bands like Rage Against the Machine and Pearl Jam, among others. "We got together, I think we did 'Into the Fire,' and he said, 'Go home, write some more of those.'"

Bruce contacted several families who had lost loved ones in the Twin Towers. He called 9/11 widows and talked with them for a long time, asking them to concerts as his guests, moved by the obituaries he'd read. "You have to be very... just very thoughtful when you're putting yourself in shoes you haven't worn," he explains. Stacey Farrelly, who was "heavily medicated" and grieving for her husband Joe, a fireman with Manhattan Engine Co. 4, received one call from Bruce. "I got through Joe's memorial and a good month and a half on that phone call," she explains.

Another woman, Suzanne Berger, lost her husband, Jim, a senior vice president at Aon Consulting who had escorted coworkers to the elevators but kept coming back around his office on the 101st floor of the south tower to ensure that everyone had gotten out. When Bruce heard in Jim's obituary that he'd been a fan, he called her; he also sent a taped greeting and a song for his memorial. "He said, 'I want to respect your privacy, but I just wanted you to know that I was very touched, and I want to know more about your husband,'" Berger explains. "He said he wanted to hear Jim's story, so I told him."

The Rising ties to Springsteen's background as well, including more overt religious symbolism, which may be important when writing about such a tragic event. His ability to decode large emotions is especially poignant here, as he transmits the vast sense of loss in the minute elements of those left behind's life. Following his characters' history, it seems to reason that some of them, or perhaps their children, would have been among the firefighters or cops who died in the Twin Towers. His "Mary" persona, a moniker he's used several times since his first album, is also back, appearing in a garden, possibly as a widow, possibly as an epiphany, and in the title of another song. "It's not necessarily the same person," he explains, "and there's a little continuum that happens for people who are watching or listening." The name floats through your body of work, leaving its own trail of where you've been and where you're going." Brendan O'Brien, the producer who helped usher Bruce into a new era, even performed glockenspiel on the record, which has been a resounding feature of his work since his early days.

The Rising achieved the near-impossible feat of producing a response to 9/11 that was empathic without being maudlin, and was never patriotic. The record was the perfect mix of tragedy, rage, love, faith, and healing. "The words felt like secrets being told," one 9/11 widow remarked. On the album, Springsteen intentionally strove to put himself in the shoes of his characters, and the result was fascinating. It was his first Billboard number one album since 1995's Greatest Hits, and it sold 525,000 copies in its first week, a career high for him. It also earned three Grammy nominations and established his third act, giving him a firm platform in the new millennium.

Chapter 9:
American Skin

Chris Christie, New Jersey's tough-talking Republican governor for the new millennium, is a big fan of Bruce Springsteen. Bruce, similarly, does not reciprocate his feelings.

Christie was born to run for office in Springsteen's and his home state, but his admiration for Bruce is not motivated by politics. It's earnest and earned, having attended over 130 performances, on his feet and singing along, knowing every lyric, feeling the same rapture as everyone else in a sea of fans. The governor before him, Wall

Street millionaire Jon Corzine, fled a Bruce performance before the encores. That was unfathomable to Christie.

He'd spent most of his life as a moderate Republican in a generally blue state, having been born in Newark and raised in a modest suburb. As he progressed through the ranks of his party, he leaned more to the right, but the Jersey homeboy he idolized as a kid remains his rock 'n' roll hero.

Springsteen, on the other hand, is out of Chris Christie's reach and uninterested in meeting. Bruce described his ideas as harmful to the poor and middle class in a letter to the editor of the Asbury Park Press. On Late Night with Jimmy Fallon, he satirized the governor's George Washington Bridge scandal, singing a "Born to Run" parody about the bridge's closure under Christie, ridiculing Christie's two-hour apology news conference ("It was longer than one of my own damn shows," Bruce sang). It took President Obama to bring the two together at a Hurricane Sandy event in New York. Christie claims he sobbed as they hugged.

Despite their similar love of a widely disliked state, Catholic upbringing, and strong Italian moms, it's hardly a surprise that Bruce has avoided the governor. Earlier in his career, he'd avoided partisan politics, whether it was as significant as refusing to allow Ronald Reagan to use "Born to Run" in his presidential campaign, or as insignificant as refusing to meet Fawn Hall backstage after a concert during the Oliver North Iran-Contra scandal. Later in his career, he'd become more political, campaigning for John Kerry and Barack Obama and writing an op-ed piece for the New York Times.

What's more puzzling is why Christie still loves Springsteen, despite their massive political differences and snubs. Their perspectives on what is best for the state and country are starkly different. "Someday, Governor, I don't know when this will all come to an end / but 'till then, you're killing the working man,' ' Bruce and Fallon sang. Yes, he's a comedian, but his values are deeply anchored in his blue-collar upbringing and fiercely reflected in the songs he's written since.

Christie's unrequited love for Bruce, though, highlights one of the most fascinating aspects of Springsteen's relationship with his followers, at least in the United States. Even those who strongly oppose his politics don't allow it to detract from their enjoyment of his CDs and, especially, his live appearances. It's remarkable in an increasingly polarized culture. Consider the Dixie Chicks, whose career came to an end when singer Natalie Maines said one sentence about George W. Bush during a concert.

Even when he was at his most vociferous, Bruce received minimal opposition. "American Skin (41 Shots)" is a film about Amadou Diallo, a twenty-two-year-old Guinean immigrant living in New York City who was assassinated by four plainclothes police officers in 1999. When the officers stopped him, Diallo withdrew his wallet from his pocket, which they mistook for a gun and opened fire. There were other songs written on the incident, but Springsteen's received the most attention. He added it to the reunion tour, which began on June 4, 2000, in Atlanta, Georgia, shortly before the band traveled north for the ten-night stand in New York City's Madison Square Garden, which was filmed for HBO. During the week between shows, a whirlwind formed, with strong ideas spoken and sides drawn.

It was a rebirth for Springsteen; he felt it was as good as his best work and helped him transition back into writing for the E Street Band. He claims he was not attempting to criticize New York police officers, but rather making a wider comment about race in America. "The first voice you hear after the intro is from the policeman's point of view," Springsteen explains. "I worked hard to achieve a balanced voice." I knew a rant would be futile. I just wanted to help people see things from the other guy's perspective." Bruce performed the song at all ten New York performances and filmed a video for it with Philadelphia collaborator Jonathan Demme during a sound check. Rather than back down from the criticism, he doubled down, adding a song called "Code of Silence" to the set he'd co written with his friend, special ed teacher and musician Joe Grushecky, which went on to earn him a Grammy for Best Solo Rock Vocal. The lyrics were about a couple splitting up, but the title related to police activity.

Bruce and Jon Bon Jovi had donated $112,000 for the family of a dead Red Bank, New Jersey, police officer just two years before. New York City Mayor Rudy Giuliani and Police Commissioner Howard Safir both condemned him. Bob Lucente, the head of the New York State Fraternal Order of Police, referred to him as a "dirtbag" and a "floating fag." (Lucente eventually apologized to homosexual police officers and resigned; Bruce later said he looked it up to figure out what it meant.) The Patrolmen's Benevolent Association called for a boycott of the shows, although few people followed through. "It's not that big of a deal. "People blow things up," says Natalie Carbone, a New Jersey-born New York City police officer and Bruce Springsteen devotee. "I don't think this will change how police officers perceive Bruce Springsteen." It's only a song."

Three years later, when NYPD Chief Joe Esposito heard Springsteen play "American Skin" at New York's Shea Stadium, followed by "Into the Fire," his post-9/11 ode to firefighters, he refused to accompany him from the stadium to the neighboring World's Fair Marina. However, the response to the song was mostly measured. It sparked debate rather than hatred. The boos were drowned out in concert by his trademark, an arena full of people yelling "Bruuuuuuce."

As the decade progressed, Springsteen became more outspoken in his songs, interviews, and beyond. His 2004 New York Times op-ed piece described his personal politics, explained why he supported John Kerry's presidential campaign, and highlighted his participation on the Vote for Change tour with the Dixie Chicks, Dave Matthews Band, and others.

"Artists and musicians play an important role in a country's social and political life." Over the years, I've tried to think long and hard about what it means to be an American: about our special identity and position in the world, and how we may effectively carry that position. I've attempted to write songs that both celebrate and condemn our successes.

"These are the central issues in this election: who we are, what we stand for, and why we fight." Personally, I have always avoided party politics during the previous 25 years. Instead, I've been political about a set of ideas, including economic fairness, civil rights, a humane foreign policy, freedom, and a decent living for all of our citizens. This year, though, the stakes have become too high for many of us to sit out the election.

"Through my art, I've always attempted to ask difficult questions. Why is it that the world's wealthiest nation finds it so difficult to fulfill its promises and faith with its most vulnerable citizens? Why is it still so difficult for us to look beyond the barrier of race? How do we behave in difficult circumstances without annihilating the things we cherish? Why does the fulfillment of our promise as a people always seem to be just around the corner but always seem to be out of reach?

Nonetheless, the guy who had spoken to and for blue-collar America for over three decades was not at odds with his audience. If you ask conservative admirers how they can stomach Springsteen's liberal politics, they'll probably answer something like, "He packs his stuff up." He incorporated charity issues into his presentations from the start and was consistently and copiously giving when confronted with genuine human need. From refusing to enter a studio if he couldn't compose music on his own terms to turning down huge offers for the use of his songs and likeness, he is resolute. Bruce won an Ellis Island Family Heritage Award from Lee Iacocca in 2010; he'd previously rejected a $12 million contract from the former Chrysler CEO to sing in a car commercial.

While some criticize Springsteen for being a workingman's poet who has never worked, it is clear that he works constantly at a profession that few could ever accomplish. He's disciplined both professionally and personally, writing and creating nonstop and preserving his physique to the point where he can do most of the things he did at thirty well into his sixties. He values family, raising three children (one of whom is now a volunteer fireman) mere minutes from his boyhood home so they could be close to his and Patti's extended family. He believes in community and refuses to live the life of a recluse rock star. He may own a $10 million home on 200 acres of prime New Jersey real estate, but he's approachable, frequently dropping in on friends' gigs at small shore clubs, taking his kids and their friends to concerts at the PNC Bank Art Center in Holmdel, performing annual benefit concerts for the Rumson Country Day School, and raving about how a new supermarket in town is his new favorite place. He traveled to the restored Winter Garden Atrium at the World Financial Center in Manhattan in 2006 to hear a group of musicians recreate songs he'd written for and during Nebraska, and he surprised the audience by jumping onstage to join the artists for the encore. Whatever he does, he does it with dedication and integrity, and he gives it his all. Vote for Change may or may not have swayed his audience, but they still adored him.

Springsteen's unusual relationship with his fans is further explored in the 2013 film Springsteen & I. The film, which is composed of home movies mixed with concert footage spanning Springsteen's career, allows fans to explain the crucial role that Springsteen plays in their lives. For the uninitiated, it also conveys some of the concert experience, such as the improvised style of the performances, the connection with the audience, and the strong sense of community. Bruce welcomes fans onstage, hugs and kisses them, dances with them, and jams with them. An Elvis impersonator known as "The Philly Elvis" recalls trying for years to sing with the E Street Band, and a video reveals the night he eventually succeeded. He sings a couple of songs with the band and overstays his welcome, but a kind Springsteen sends him on his way with the classic "Elvis has left the building."

People look to Bruce and his music for advice (as depicted in High Fidelity), life lessons, and solace through terrible times. "He taught me how to be a decent man," claims one fan. The film explains Springsteen's unique ability to express knowledge through his engagement with his audience. A young fan with a hi bruce, i just got dumped, i'm goin down a placard piques Springsteen's curiosity at a show in Canada. "What exactly happened, bro?" Springsteen asks, dropping his microphone and waiting for the man to respond. "She didn't think I was spending enough time with her," says the sign holder. "You probably weren't!" Springsteen's unique giggle is mimicked by the audience. When the young man requests a hug, Bruce says, "Get on up here," and embraces him. "Everything will be fine," he says. "I've been dumped numerous times... They're kicking themselves now! They left too quickly! They missed that record company advance," he says, making a passing reference to his song "Rosalita" before launching into the fan's request.

The film briefly touches on the worldwide Springsteen phenomenon, where he's an even bigger success outside of his own country, and highlights it through amusing translation errors. A middle-aged Danish woman claims Bruce has been her friend since 1985, despite the fact that he is unaware of this. She wishes she had the "love" he describes in "Red Headed Woman," a song about oral sex, and says it would be lovely to be loved like that. Misinterpreting the words of the song "Born in the U.S.A." causes a Polish native to idealize America over his torn country. "You are the guide of my life," a young Japanese girl says of Bruce. A mysterious individual upgrades an English factory worker who has been saving for twenty years to travel New York and witness a Bruce performance from the nosebleed section to the front row.

Baillie Walsh asks fans to characterize Springsteen in three words, an effective shortcut for demystifying the rock star's impact on actual lives—"hope," "togetherness," "passionate," "energy," and "power," among many others—and then delivers sincere, tear-jerking tributes to him. Most importantly, they communicate the intimacy that Springsteen delivers in an arena environment, a talent that is unrivaled. "I felt like I was the only one there," recalls one enthusiast. "It felt like he was singing just for me." The personal experiences and comments aren't stalkerish, but they do communicate that these people spend a lot of time listening to Bruce's music, and that the uplifting quality of it is addictive.

Fans appeared to follow Springsteen wherever he went by 2005, and he had another challenge for them: his thirteenth studio album, Devils & Dust. It was raw and grim, like Nebraska and The Ghost of Tom Joad, and primarily performed by Bruce himself, as was the solo tour he embarked on to support it. The songs, some of which he'd written after shows on the Joad tour, fit beautifully into the news cycle at the time, as he fell back into character and sang about someone else's life. In the eponymous tune, he explores the personal toll of the Iraq war on those who fought in it. He follows the movements of an undocumented immigrant in the style of Sunset Boulevard, beginning with the man dying in the river ("Matamoros Banks")—a successor, he claims, to Joad's "Across the Border." He's a lad whose mother dies, and he imagines her spirit as a horse ("Silver Palomino"), a song he says was inspired by a friend of his and Patti's who had passed away with young children. He pays a despondent, explicit visit to a prostitute ("Reno") and drops the F-bomb ("Long Time Comin'"), neither of which he'd ever done in song before.

Bruce claims producer Brendan O'Brien helped him find out the best approach to deliver the material in the studio, minimalist and twangy with just enough accompaniment. He rehearsed with a few musicians for the tour (at the Asbury Park boardwalk's Paramount Theater) before deciding to go it alone at venues with up to 5,000 seats. As a fascinating acoustic performer—a skill that drew him in to begin with—the solo gigs allowed for even more storytelling from the stage. On the Devils tour, he joked about the stages of parenthood, from when children are little and their parents are their entire universe through the adolescent years when "they think you're an idiot," he added. He used "Racing in the Street" to refer to Two-Lane Blacktop, a 1970s road movie starring Beach Boys drummer Dennis Wilson and a youthful James Taylor (with a full head of hair). In St. Paul, Minnesota, he dedicated "A Good Man Is Hard to Find" to deceased officer Sergeant Gerald Vick. He dedicated "Land of Hope and Dreams" to numerous city food banks. He tested himself by playing the piano, which had not always gone well in the past, but he returned to it.

And, for a little period, he returned to partisan politics, opening "Part Man, Part Monkey" with a question on whether Karl Rove and George W. Bush believe in evolution. (W. had expressed skepticism.) Bruce frowned when his banter earned applause. "I don't want to feel like I'm preaching to the choir, that's a pretty hack," he said. "During the election, I received a lot of negative messages, and those are the ones I enjoy... It lets you know you've struck a nerve... My personal favorite was a couple of boxes of crushed records and a dead chicken... That was a lovely touch, in my opinion... But how did they get those records?

Chapter 10:
American Skin

During the E Street Band's 1999-2000 reunion tour, Bruce ended each set with an emotionally charged rendition of "If I Should Fall Behind," a meditation on love and how it might linger or last. Each band member stood up and sang with Bruce, one by one. Nils Lofgren reminded us how talented he is as a singer. Patti Scialfa's soulful vibrato was stunning. But, with Bruce present, Danny Federici's and Clarence Clemons' turns at the microphone were mournful and foreboding: "I'll wait for you / And if I should fall behind / Wait for me."

Both men died as Springsteen entered his adolescence in the new millennium, Federici in 2008 and Clemons in 2011. Terry Magovern, his friend and personal helper, died in 2007 (fans at Tunnel of Love Express events saw him onstage as the man in the carnival ticket office; Bruce wrote "Terry's Song" for him), and his trainer Tony Strollo died in 2012. (Springsteen startled the entire town of Asbury Park by performing an unexpected concert at a benefit for Strollo's young children.)

These losses came during a moment of significant artistic progress and recognition for Springsteen. He was writing and recording more prolifically and successfully, expanding his sound pallet. For years, he had addressed the repercussions of war and immigration difficulties, but now he was becoming increasingly vocal about his views on American politics, the expanding income disparity, and other economic woes. His albums continued to chart at number one. He received the Kennedy Center Honors. Just a few weeks after performing at the president's inauguration, he and the E Street Band performed a Super Bowl halftime extravaganza that spanned four decades in twelve minutes. He delivered an amazing keynote presentation at SXSW, the annual music and film festival in Austin, Texas. He became the first musician in four decades to have four number one singles. The hard-rocking disappointment of 2007's Magic and the denunciation of Wall Street greed in 2012's Wrecking Ball echoed the United States' economic downturn and the banking crises for which no one was held accountable. This period was also marked by bereavements.

It's very uncommon for friends and loved ones to drift apart over time, but playing together would never be the same for the E Street Band. Springsteen included tracks that Federici and Clemons had left in the mix on the albums he recorded after they were gone. However, when the band was inducted into the Rock and Roll Hall of Fame in 2014, their absence cut a bittersweet streak through the acclaim of finally being acknowledged by the Hall with Bruce. Photos of the two, as well as a cassette clip of the Big Man humming a melody (performed by his widow, Victoria, who accepted on his behalf), elicited strong emotions. Springsteen's one regret was that it happened after they were gone, he added as he inducted all of his bandmates, past and present, in his intimate, conversational style.

It's apt that Bruce's 2014 collection of covers and re-recorded material, High Hopes, offers a look back mixed with forward momentum. He reinvents The Rising outtakes ("Harry's Place," "Down in the Hole") and resurrects "American Skin (41 Shots)" and "The Ghost of Tom Joad." "Frankie Fell in Love" sounds like it could have come from the 2006 Seeger Sessions, while "Heaven's Wall" may have come from Wrecking Ball. And he revisits his appreciation of punk rock, hearkening back to the New York City nights of the early 1970s when he'd miss the last bus back to Asbury Park and pass the time at Max's Kansas City, watching bands like the New York Dolls and Suicide until dawn; he covers Suicide's "Dream Baby Dream" and "Just Like Fire Would" by the Saints, a criminally underappreciated Australian band of the 1970s that, like Bruce, added a horn section to their rock 'n' roll.

The title tune of High Hopes, written by roots rocker Tim Scott McConnell, was originally recorded by Springsteen with the E Street Band during their brief reunion in 1995 on his Blood Brothers EP. Rage Against the Machine guitarist Tom Morello, a Springsteen friend and collaborator since 2008, discovered the uncommon music on Sirius XM's E Street Radio one night and brought it to Springsteen's notice. Bruce added the song to the set list after hearing the request, and they recorded it while on tour in Australia, when

Morello was filling in for Steven Van Zandt (who was busy working on his excellent TV series Lilyhammer). Morello, who also appeared on Springsteen's 2012 album Wrecking Ball, said the sessions were so impromptu that he wasn't convinced they were working on a major release. However, as Bruce's inspiration swelled, his eighteenth studio album, and eleventh number one, fell into shape around its title track. "We've never had a recording session during a tour in our lives," he explains. "We did a few things that I wanted to document. So that was thrilling. It was also exciting to be with Tommy. The band—Steven, Nils, and the rest of the guys—remains an inspiration to me."

Morello and Springsteen are the most likely of friends, despite their shared political ideals and diverse musical output. Morello, who has courted controversy with ideological pronouncements at times, and Springsteen, who has avoided party politics for much of his career, appear to be significant influences on one another. Morello revitalizes Springsteen. "Tom and his guitar became my muse, pushing the rest of this project to another level," Bruce wrote in the album's liner notes. In exchange, he increased Morello's repertoire (the 2013 tour comprised 223 different songs), as well as putting him through the paces of a three-and-a-half-hour act. Morello, the lead guitarist for Rage, says he'd never sang with an electric guitar in his hands until he joined Springsteen onstage for "The Ghost of Tom Joad" at the Pond in Anaheim in 2008. (A decade earlier, Rage had released a thrash-rap rendition of the song.) Bruce was so taken with what Morello did to the song that he re-recorded it with Tom for High Hopes.

"The Ghost of Tom Joad," like the John Steinbeck figure who inspired it, is as timely as ever. "I think it was one of Bruce's best songs, and it really cuts to the core of his social justice writing in a way that tells a story," Morello said of the song. "The song tells a very human story, and the musical accompaniment invokes two very different ends of the spectrum of social justice struggle." There's a somber ballad that sounds like a lament. There's also the full-bore rocker, which feels like a danger."

Springsteen's humanity is part of what makes his songs ageless and so universally relatable to crises and injustice. He dedicated "American Skin (41 Shots)" in concert to Trayvon Martin, the seventeen-year-old who was shot dead in Florida by neighborhood watchman George Zimmerman, who was ultimately acquitted of murder. He revived "My City of Ruins" for his post-Katrina performance in New Orleans eight months after the devastation. It was the Jazz and Heritage Festival's first night of the 2006 Seeger Sessions tour, a vast cabal of artists he'd collected to play traditional tunes popularized by folk singer and activist Pete Seeger. Bruce didn't hide his dissatisfaction with the government, dedicating "How Can a Poor Man Stand Such Times and Live?" to "President Bystander" (a reference to George W. Bush, who was severely condemned for his handling of the tragedy) and included local references in a verse:

"There's bodies floatin' on the canal and the levees gone to hell / Them who've gotten out of town and them who ain't got left to drown."
It was Bruce's Jazz Fest debut; perhaps he knew the people of New Orleans needed him, and he expressed their agony and despair. "I saw sights I never thought I'd see in an American city," he said from the Ninth Ward, the area of the city severely damaged by the hurricane. "You're enraged by the criminal ineptitude."

Although the first gig demanded moral anger, The Seeger Sessions was a more joyous undertaking. Devils & Dust felt like a foreboding reaction to a second Bush term. This initiative epitomized Seeger's more optimistic spirit, or, as Springsteen called it at Seeger's 90th birthday celebration event at Madison Square Garden, his "stubborn, defiant, and nasty optimism." But Bruce was also a fan of the music. In some ways, the project had progressed slowly. Springsteen had recorded "We Shall Overcome" for a tribute album in 1997 and had begun to explore Seeger's works. When putting the project together, he contacted various musicians he'd informally jammed with over the years. It developed to include anywhere from seventeen to twenty pickers and grinners armed with stringed instruments, horns, and percussion. After all, Springsteen had assembled Dr. Zoom and the Sonic Boom with multiple instrumentalists of all types and had a ten-piece, eponymously named ensemble before being signed as a solo artist. We Shall Overcome: The Seeger Sessions, the CD he created with his new band, is an upbeat hootenanny, a roaring celebration of Seeger's plain, sing-along folk song. The album tour continued in a similar vein—not a terrible way to see out the administration against which Bruce had fought.

Barack Obama, the man he campaigned for, was sworn in as the 44th President of the United States in 2009. Springsteen and Seeger sang Woody Guthrie's "This Land Is Your Land" at the inauguration, with Seeger insisting on singing all of the lyrics. Later that year, at Pete's ninetieth birthday party, Bruce discussed the journey in terms of what Seeger meant to him and the nation:

"While Pete and I were on our way to Washington for President Obama's inaugural celebration, he gave me the entire tale of 'We Shall Overcome.' It evolved from a labor movement song to a civil rights movement song thanks to Pete's influence. That day, when we sang 'This Land Is Your Land,' I looked at Pete, the first black president of the United States, who was seated on his right, and I reflected on Pete's tremendous journey. My own upbringing in the 1960s in cities scarred by racial violence made that time seem almost unreal, yet Pete had thirty years of struggle and serious activism under his belt... Pete Seeger wanted to become a walking, singing reminder of all of America's past at some point. He'd be a living record of America's music and conscience, a witness to song and culture's power to prod history along, to drive American events toward more compassionate and justified ends."

Springsteen, a longstanding Woody Guthrie lover, had overlooked Seeger for a long time, discovering the folk singer later in life, but their common ground was obvious. He and Seeger were both elected to the American Academy of Arts and Sciences in 2013—two of just nine people in the "Performing Arts—Criticism and Practice" category (Robert De Niro and Herbie Hancock were also among them). Seeger died three months later, at the age of ninety-four.

Loss was never far from Springsteen throughout these years, and it washed over his beloved Asbury Park in October 2012. Hurricane

Sandy was one of the most powerful storms to have hit the Atlantic Ocean. It gained power as it proceeded north on the Gulf Stream until it was redirected sharply to the left by a high-pressure air mass from Canada. It hit the Jersey Shore, devastating lengths of boardwalk, beaches, residences, businesses, restaurants, pubs, and amusement parks like the one Bruce described in "Born to Run." It swept a foot of sand into Convention Hall, the venue of many of Bruce Springsteen's international tour rehearsals.

Bruce, a native and lifelong resident, immediately recognized what had been lost—not just the memories of many children who grew up in New Jersey and spent their summers on the coast, but also a destination that had been affordable and accessible, and might no longer be in the aftermath of the storm. "The Jersey Coast had a very unique personality," he adds, "some places with well-to-do people, some places with a lot of working-class people and middle-class people who could have homes." So seeing it washed away was excruciating."

Springsteen was the first to agree to participate in an instant telethon to collect funds for catastrophe victims. Hurricane Sandy: Coming Together aired on NBC without commercials just two days after the storm passed. Christina Aguilera, Billy Joel, Mary J. Blige, and Jon Bon Jovi gathered in Studio 6A at 30 Rock in New York City and raised more than $23 million for the Red Cross. Bruce ended the night with "Land of Hope and Dreams," which transitioned into "People Get Ready," as it often did.

The Concert for Sandy Relief, a six-hour event performed at Madison Square Garden, featured the Rolling Stones, the Who, Paul McCartney, Dave Grohl, Kanye West, and many other artists. All earnings went to the Robin Hood Foundation, a non-profit that fights poverty. This time, the E Street Band opened the night with "Land of Hope and Dreams," "Wrecking Ball," and, of course, "My City of Ruins," his Asbury Park lament, before concluding with a special appearance by Jon Bon Jovi on "Born to Run."

However, Springsteen marketed Wrecking Ball and High Hopes with tours outside of the United States for the entirety of 2013 and the first quarter of 2014. Since the days of Born in the USA, his international fan base has overtaken his committed American fan base in intensity. His 1988 performance at the Radrennbahn Weissensee in East Berlin gathered 160,000 people, the highest crowd the venue has ever seen. Springsteen famously stated, "I'm not here to support or oppose any particular government, but to play rock 'n' roll for [you] East Berliners... in the hope that one day, all barriers will be torn down." The Berlin Wall was demolished the next year.

Europeans have long admired rock, country, and blues music from the United States. They have a soft spot for socially conscientious Americans, of whom Springsteen is clearly one. But it goes beyond that. His European audience is younger than his American audience. They don't stick to Springsteen's historical touchstones, and hence lack certain American audience expectations. They were either born after the 1970s or were not as familiar with Bruce as many of his American followers were. They embrace new material, as opposed to those who want to hear staples like "Born to Run." Some of these countries' economic troubles have affected their youth especially hard, making his recent songs even more popular. And the locations he sings about—the Jersey Shore in his early work, the Southwest in his latter work—are foreign to them.

According to Bruce, European fans have an emotional openness that is uncommon in the United States. They are more enthusiastic about him. In Milan, Italy, he was greeted by a billboard that read: LAST WEEK THE POPE ARRIVED, NEXT WEEK MADONNA, BUT GOD IS HERE... NOW. During a concert in Gothenburg, Sweden, a feverish audience caused structural damage to the arena, putting Springsteen on the front pages of newspapers. Filling a fifty-thousand-seat arena represents a considerable portion of the local population in smaller communities, making an E Street Band tour such an important event that practically everything closes for the night.

And the hand-hewn placards that audience members wave to request a song, send Bruce a message, or ask a question are as accessible as the crowds. Springsteen went into European audiences virtually every night, picking the more unique ones, from the sacred to the profane, and challenged himself and his band to perform the demands. A fan's handmade placard in Hannover, Germany, offers a trade for a request: I'd give my right testicle to hear drift away, a dobie gray cover. "I'll play 'drift away,'" Bruce said, "as long as I don't have to see either the left or right testicle."

Springsteen has been performing music for nearly fifty years and shows no signs of slowing down. He's continuously pushing his creative boundaries, co-directing a ten-minute video with longtime documentarian Thom Zimny as a companion piece to High Hopes' post-apocalyptic "Hunter of Invisible Game." He also made his acting debut as a mortician and hit man in the season three finale of Lilyhammer, directed by Steve Van Zandt. He can still tour, play big shows, climb up on top of pianos, and crowd-surf like he has always done because of a dedication to fitness and the luck of a gene pool jackpot. What began as an obsession for him has evolved into a calling, and the calling would not exist without that interaction. He emphasized his dedication to his audience in 1985. "That ticket is my handshake," he declared. "That ticket is me promising you that I'll go all the way every time." That is my agreement.``

It's still a contract, and he's just as enthused about it as he was before, if not more. In mid-2014, he posted a thank-you note to fans who came out to see him on the Wrecking Ball and High Hopes tours, as well as the film he made with Zimny:

"The last two years and nearly 170 shows have changed my life." We have lived deep within the transforming force of rock 'n' roll thanks to you. You've aided in the formation of a new and revitalized E Street Band. We enter this hiatus with a renewed sense of purpose and the spirit to bring you our best in the future."

Chapter 11:
New York City Serenade

President Barack Obama bestowed the Medal of Freedom on Bruce Springsteen in November 2016, praising him for his poetic portrayal of "the simple glories and scattered heartbreak of everyday life in America," as well as the challenge he poses through his music and activism, "... asking us all, 'What is the work for us to do in our short time here?'"

The last was a contemplative inquiry posed by the President, whose presidency was drawing to an end. Nearly eight years earlier, at Obama's star-studded, inspirational "We Are One" inauguration, Bruce stepped in front of the Lincoln Memorial and sang "The Rising" with his acoustic guitar and the Joyce Garrett Singers, a huge gospel choir. Springsteen wanted to do something to show his appreciation during the administration's final days.

Bruce performed a secret gig in the East Room for the Obamas and their staff on January 12, 2017, two days after the President's farewell address. What began with one acoustic guitar ended with another. Bruce's fifteen-song solo set was appropriately melancholy and contemplative, complementing the night's era-ending vibe. Between songs, he talked about nation and family—both the first family and his own—inviting his wife, fellow E Street Band member Patti Scialfa, to join him on two songs. The compilation included songs ranging from Greetings from Asbury Park's "Growin' Up" to Wrecking Ball's "Land of Hope and Dreams," as well as Tunnel of Love outtake "The Wish" and his Grammy Award-winning "Devils & Dust."

The private concert was more than simply a consolation prize for the people he'd campaigned with and cared about for the previous eight years. It aided in crystallizing an idea Bruce had for a different type of show. Storytelling had always been a feature of his epic concerts, but he had begun to imagine a solo performance in which the stories took center stage. Not a solo acoustic, three-thousand-seat theater tour like he'd done in promotion of The Ghost of Tom Joad and Devils & Dust, nor a scaled-down version of his massive rock act. This would be a (largely) one-man show in an even smaller venue, exquisite but austere, with just guitars, piano, and Patti on a couple of songs. It was the birth of Bruce Springsteen on Broadway.

Bruce chose the Walter Kerr Theatre, located at 219 West 48th Street, between Seventh and Eighth Avenues in New York's famous Theater District, after meticulously inspecting playhouses from every conceivable viewpoint. The theater, an Adamesque structure established in 1921, is one of the area's most intimate venues, with fewer than a thousand seats. Bette Davis and Helen Hayes performed on its stage when it was known as The Ritz, and it later became a radio and television studio in the 1940s. After lying dormant for many years, it was meticulously restored to its original golden "glory days," right down to the incandescent light fittings, in the 1980s. Walter Kerr was a brilliant pick for Bruce Springsteen. The provocative, award-winning play Angels in America premiered in 1993, the same year Bruce recorded his Oscar, Golden Globe, and four-time Grammy-winning song "Streets of Philadelphia" for the film Philadelphia, which also chronicled the deadliest days of the AIDS epidemic.

Springsteen on Broadway began previews on October 3, 2017, with Bruce dedicating the first performance to his buddy Tom Petty, who died unexpectedly the night before at the age of sixty-six. On October 12, 2017, the show debuted. It was certain to be a blockbuster at such a small theater, but it was an outright smash, grossing $2.33 million in its first week of sales and breaking Hamilton's record for average ticket price. The show was so popular that he extended the original limited run from November to February 2018, then again from June to December 2018.

The fifteen-song show, which included many songs from his East Room setlist, lasted around two hours and included no intermission. Bruce worked as his own writer and director, remaining in complete control of his music and narrative. His talking troubadour method was given a theatrical sense by the austere stage and sometimes-shadowy lighting, with the "talking" taking up more than half of the performance, allowing an opportunity to explicate his life and work. This presentation highlighted more of what pushed him to do what inspired his work for nearly five decades, without the happy gloss of great musical arrangements. "Dancing in the Dark" emphasized how the rock celebrity failed to cure his psychic wounds. "Tenth Avenue Freeze Out" honored his buddy Clarence Clemons while emphasizing that death is never something you get over, rather something you learn to live with. He dispelled the myth that "Born in the U.S.A." is a dogmatic flag-waver rather than the protest song spelt out in the lyrics for anyone who still believes it is. He delved into the thorny nature of love and commitment, with Patti accompanying him on "Tougher Than the Rest" and "Brilliant Disguise." And he took the small audience on a tour of his boyhood in Freehold, New Jersey, with songs like "My Hometown" and "My Father's House."

Since shortly after his first performance on that chilly January day in 2009, the plan for Springsteen on Broadway has been evolving for years. The following month, as Bruce and the E Street Band prepared to perform the Super Bowl XLIII Halftime Show, the singer/songwriter became a temporary blogger, chronicling the mechanics of a gig with a worldwide audience of 100 million or so. Bruce discovered a fresh writing voice that piqued his interest, so he continued to write. Born to Run, his book, was released in September 2016. Springsteen's book is 508 pages long, as one would anticipate from a musician whose concerts last more than three hours. His familiar tone, both engaging and self-deprecating, as well as concise chapters and rich images, keep it going like a live concert.

Born to Run dives into the melancholy that drives Bruce's songs and his "workaholism." Some of it is old territory for fans, ranging from his tense relationship with his father and conflicting thoughts about faith, to his Jersey Shore upbringing and bandmates and pals. However, the book weaves familiar and fresh experiences into a narrative arc that better defines Springsteen: the man and the artist. He apologizes for his first marriage and other romantic disasters. He discusses the intensity of his anxiousness as a child, as well as the sadness that afflicted him well into his sixties. Its companion album, Chapter and Verse, begins with rare tunes from his Castiles and Steel Mill days, but it was the audiobook version of Born to Run, read by Bruce himself, that received a Grammy nomination for Best Spoken Word in 2018.

Springsteen honored the 35th anniversary of his first number-one album with an enhanced reissue: The Ties That Bind: The River

Collection box set (published December 2015), while working on his gigantic memoir. Taking the E Street Band across the world during 2016, they had the highest-grossing global tour of the year, breaking Taylor Swift's all-time record.

Bruce broke his own record just one month before his 67th birthday. It was the first night of the tour's second U.S. leg, a homecoming at MetLife Stadium in Secaucus, New Jersey, on August 23, 2016. He and the band began with "New York City Serenade" from The Wild, the Innocent, and the E Street Shuffle, accompanied by a string section. They had tried it in Europe over the summer, but it became the official opening song of that leg of the tour that night. Then, in the wetlands of the Meadowlands, Springsteen performed for three hours and fifty-two minutes, his longest U.S. show to date. Governor Christie, dressed in khaki shorts, sat in a stadium box above the majority of the throng. (Always a fan, Christie sat in the second row at Springsteen on Broadway on his first night out of office, January 18, 2018.)

Bruce bested himself again two nights later on the same site, clocking in at three hours and fifty-nine minutes. On August 30, 2016, he completed his Jersey trifecta by breaking four hours. The next week, he gave a four-hour-and-four-minute concert in Philadelphia, falling just two minutes short of his career-high in Helsinki, Finland, in 2012.

With the public's desire for live performance recordings growing, Springsteen continues to add to the career-spanning collection he started in 2014. He has also utilized it to help others. During the 2017 hurricanes Harvey and Irma, he donated the revenues from an archival Houston show from 1978's Darkness on the Edge of Town tour to the MusiCares Hurricane Relief Fund to assist catastrophe victims in Texas and Florida.

Another, more substantial collection, which had been held at the Asbury Park Public Library, acquired a larger, permanent home at Monmouth University in West Long Branch, New Jersey. It's only two miles from Bruce's birthplace and one mile from the leased house where he wrote "Born to Run" on the eve of rock 'n' roll legend. The Bruce Springsteen Archives and Center for American Music presently houses the singer's personal archives and hosts events such as the April 2018 "Darkness on the Edge of Town: An International Symposium."

Springsteen is one of the rare musicians who can move forward while looking back. His work depicts characters from a specific time and place, yet it is also timeless and infinitely relatable. His unwavering will to create is inspiring, but it is the humanity and decency of his lyrics that gives us hope. During the Medal of Freedom ceremony, President Obama summed up Bruce's music's continuing appeal:

"These are all anthems of our America, the reality of who we are and the reverie of who we want to be."

Printed in Great Britain
by Amazon

50332502R00048